Special Happenings

Special Happenings

Eldonna L. Evertts / Language Arts
Lyman C. Hunt / Reading
Bernard J. Weiss / Linguistics and Curriculum

Edited by Jane Berkowitz and Craig Bettinger
Educational Consultants: Patsy Montague and Janet Sprout

THE HOLT BASIC READING SYSTEM
· LEVEL 12 ·

HOLT, RINEHART AND WINSTON, INC.
New York / Toronto / London / Sydney

Illustrated by

Bernard Waber, pages 16-35; Ethel Gold, pages 36-45; Bill Morrison, pages 46-56; Arthur Decker, pages 57, 69, 168-180; Kenneth Longtemps, pages 58-68, 280-296; Richard Amundsen, pages 70-84; Blair Drawson, pages 85, 107, 139; Colos, pages 86-95; Albert John Pucci, pages 96-106; Reynold Ruffins, pages 110-117; Bryant Weintraub, pages 118, 120, 121, 125; Carolyn Schumsky, page 119; Howard Schumsky, page 122; Holden Weintraub, pages 123, 124, 127; Norman La Liberté, pages 128-138; Lawrence Di Fiori, pages 140-151; Bob Goldstein, pages 153, 167; Norman Green, pages 154-166; Diane de Groat, pages 152, 181, 184-191, 201, 220-221, 298-311; Tad Krumeich, pages 192, 258; Marie Michal, pages 202-211; Don Freeman, pages 212-219; Lionel Kalish, pages 222-230; Jerry Zimmerman, page 231; MAGNUM: Elliott Erwitt, pages 232, 235, 245 (bottom); Wayne Miller, pages 233, 238 (left), 239, 241, 244, 245 (top); Dennis Stock, pages 234, 242; Bruce Davidson, pages 236, 243; Martin J. Dain, page 238 (right); Arthur Shilstone, pages 248-257; Denver Gillen, pages 259-265; Ingbet, pages 266-267, 297; Bill Basso, pages 268-279; Errol le Cain, pages 312-323; Edward Gorey, pages 324-351.
Cover designed by Kay Wanous; cover, pages 6-15, 108-109, 182-183, and 246-247 constructed by S. N. Studio.

Acknowledgments

Grateful acknowledgment is given to the following authors and publishers:
Abingdon Press, for "Who's There," from *Scary Things* by Norah Smaridge, copyright © 1969 by Abingdon Press; for "The Wind Came Running," from *I Rode the Black Horse Far Away* by Ivy O. Eastwick, copyright © 1960 by Abingdon Press. Used by permission.
Addison-Wesley Publishing Company, for "Kiya the Gull," adapted from *Kiya the Gull* by Fen H. Lasell. Copyright © 1969 by Fen H. Lasell. An Addisonian Press Book. Used by permission.
Atheneum Publishers, Inc., for "Today Has a Secret," from *8 A.M. Shadows* by Patricia Hubbell. Copyright © 1965 by Patricia Hubbell. Used by permission.
Atheneum Publishers, Inc., and Brandt and Brandt, for "The Bat," from *Cats and Bats and Things with Wings* by Conrad Aiken. Copyright © 1965 by Conrad Aiken. Used by permission.
Atheneum Publishers, Inc., and Angus & Robertson, for "The Royal Tailor," from *The Ombley-Gombley* by Peter Wesley-Smith and David Fielding. Copyright © 1969 by Peter Wesley-Smith and David Fielding. Used by permission.
Childrens Press, Regensteiner Publishing Enterprises, Inc., and Annette Betz, for "If I Were," by Lene Hille-Brandts, adapted by Elizabeth Duckworth from *Wenn Ich Ein Kleiner Daumling War* by Lene Hille-Brandts. Copyright © 1966 by Annette Betz. Used by permission.
Thomas Y. Crowell Company, Inc., for "Footprints," from *Feathered Ones and Furry* by Aileen Fisher. Copyright © 1971 by Aileen Fisher. Used by permission.
The John Day Company, Inc., for "Let Me Tell You About My Dad," adapted from *Let Me Tell You About My Dad* by Phillip Viereck. Copyright © 1971 by Phillip and Ellen Viereck. Used by permission.
Doubleday & Company, Inc., and Collins-Knowlton-Wing, for "The Haunted Spy," adapted from *The Haunted Spy* by Barbara Ninde Byfield. Copyright © 1969 by Barbara Ninde Byfield. Used by permission.
Follett Publishing Company, division of Follett Corporation, for "When Something Happy Happens," from *That Was Summer* by Marci Ridlon, copyright © 1969 by Marci Ridlon; for

Contents

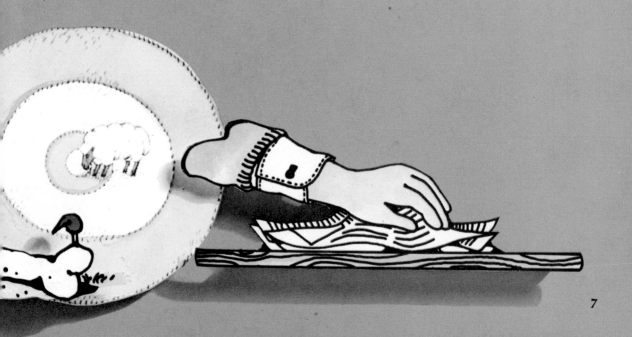

Stories and Storytellers

Artists and Performers

Special Happenings

Whispers and Secrets

Today Has a Secret

Today has a secret
Nobody knows—
Where it came from,
Where it goes.

Tomorrow won't tell you,
Today won't say,
Yesterday, yesterday,
Gone away.

Today is the secret
Today alone knows—
Where it came from,
Where it goes.

—*Patricia Hubbell*

Lovable Lyle

Bernard Waber

Everyone loved Lyle the Crocodile. The Primm family, with whom he lived, loved him dearly, of course. The lady at the store loved him. She always gave Lyle cookies. The ice cream man loved him. He always invited Lyle to climb on his truck and ring the bell. Bird loved him. *"Love Lyle! Love Lyle!"* he called. And the children loved him. They always called for Lyle to come out and play.

In return, Lyle loved the whole, wide, wonderful world. He didn't have one enemy in it . . . or so he thought.

Then one day, quite mysteriously, a note addressed to Lyle was slid under the door of the house on East 88th Street. Mr. Primm read the note to Lyle.

Dear Lyle,

    I hate you. I hate you more than anything. I hate you so much I can't stand it.

                           Your enemy

Everyone was so surprised. *"Oh, how awful!"* cried Mrs. Primm. "Why would anyone hate Lyle?"

"Don't worry about it, Lyle," said Mr. Primm. "Just keep being your wonderful self, and try to forget this ever happened."

Lyle went off to bed that night trying hard to forget. Still, as he turned off the lights and looked down upon the quiet street below, he could not help sadly thinking,

"Someone out there hates me."

The next day Lyle lost himself in play and forgot all about the note. But then a second one came as mysteriously as the first.

Dear Lyle,

I hate you even more today than I did yesterday.

Your enemy

"Oh, these horrible notes have just got to stop!" Mrs. Primm cried out.

Lyle wanted the notes stopped, too. He was very unhappy about them. Some days he just wouldn't go out of the house. Other days he stayed outside being friendly to everyone, so that somewhere, somehow, his *"enemy"* would see what a nice crocodile he really was. He smiled a big, big smile. And he waved big, big waves, calling to one and all as friendly as he knew how.

He was kind and polite. He held doors open for people with heavy bundles. He shared his umbrella.

"My, isn't he polite!" one lady said.

"I've never seen anything like it," answered another.

Poor Lyle worked so hard at being nice that he was very tired by the end of the day.

One afternoon, Mrs. Primm, Joshua, and Lyle came across the words, "Down with all crocodiles," written on a fence near East 88th Street. Mrs. Primm tried to wash off the horrible words with her handkerchief.

"Well, Lyle," she said, as they made their way home, "it seems no matter how much we may think we want to, we can't always please everyone, or be liked by everyone."

As they got near their house, they noticed Clover Sue Hipple, a new girl in the neighborhood. By the time they reached their door, Clover was gone. Resting under the door was still another note addressed to Lyle.

"I just don't know if I can bring myself to read it," said Mrs. Primm. But she did.

Dear Lyle,

I wish you would go away and never come back—ever, ever again.

Your enemy

Sadly, Mrs. Primm tore up the note.

During the next few days, Mrs. Primm and Lyle found themselves running into Clover Sue Hipple almost everywhere they went. At the grocery they found her looking out from a large pile of potatoes.

Another time they caught sight of her behind a tree. And again one afternoon, they found her behind a mailbox.

Each time, Mrs. Primm smiled and tried to say hello. And each time, Clover ran off before Mrs. Primm got to her.

One day, as she was about to leave the house, Mrs. Primm looked down just in time to see another note being pushed under the door. Quickly, she opened the door. Before her, eyes wide with surprise, and still holding the note, stood Clover Sue Hipple.

"Clover dear, please don't run away," cried Mrs. Primm. "I would like to speak with you . . . about Lyle. Has Lyle done something to make you angry with him?"

"He takes my friends away from me," the little girl said. "When Lyle comes out, my friends

run away. They run to play with him. I never have any fun when Lyle is around."

"But why can't you play with Lyle, too?" asked Mrs. Primm.

"Because I'm not allowed. My mother said I'm not allowed ever to play with *crocodiles*," said Clover.

That night Mr. Primm said, "Why don't you ask Mrs. Hipple over here to meet Lyle? I'm sure when she sees for herself how gentle Lyle really is, she won't mind if Clover plays with him."

Mrs. Primm called Clover's mother the very next day. "Lyle and I want so much to meet you," she said. "Could you join us for tea tomorrow afternoon?"

"I would love to," answered Mrs. Hipple. She made a note of the address.

"Now who is this nice Mrs. Primm?" she wondered. "And who is Lyle?" The only Lyle she knew of was that awful crocodile, who lived with a strange family somewhere nearby.

"Just think, a crocodile living right here in our neighborhood! This Lyle must be that nice Mrs. Primm's husband," she thought.

"Remember now, Lyle," said Mrs. Primm, the next afternoon, "be polite when Mrs. Hipple gets here. Take her coat. And when you have hung it in the closet, join us in the living room."

When Mrs. Hipple got there, Lyle started down the stairs to meet her. But then he stopped.

"What if she doesn't like me?" he thought. Suddenly Lyle became very shy. Suddenly the last thing in the world he wanted to do was meet Mrs. Hipple.

"Lyle! Lyle!" called Mrs. Primm. "Where are you? Mrs. Hipple is here." She led her guest into the living room.

Lyle wanted to go with her, but instead he squeezed himself into the hall closet and hid.

Over the tinkling of teacups, Lyle could hear the voices of the two women. They were talking about this, that, and everything under the sun. It was so stuffy in the closet, he began to wish they would talk about Mrs. Hipple going home soon.

At long last Lyle heard Mrs. Hipple say, "I must be going now." And Mrs. Primm said, "I'm so glad you came, and so sorry you missed Lyle, but I'm sure you will be meeting him soon." Then Lyle heard the handle of the closet door turn as Mrs. Primm said, "Here, let me get your coat."

The second the door opened, Lyle fell out upon the two women. Mrs. Primm gasped. And Mrs. Hipple yelled.

"Are you all right? Are you all right?" Mrs. Primm cried out, as they got to their feet.

"LET ME OUT OF HERE!"
Mrs. Hipple cried.
"LET ME OUT OF
THIS HORRIBLE HOUSE!"

Mrs. Primm opened the door as Mrs. Hipple, her hair and clothes all a mess, ran from the house. "If that crocodile ever so much as crosses my path, I'll have him put in jail," she called back over her shoulder.

"Poor Lyle," Mrs. Primm said that night. "Now he's afraid he's going to be put in jail. We're just going to have to think of something to take his mind off his troubles."

On the first warm day, Mr. and Mrs. Primm knew just what to do for Lyle. "We'll take him to the beach," they thought.

Lyle always loved to swim. And he could swim better than anyone in the family.

While Mr. and Mrs. Primm sat down on the beach, and Joshua started on a sand castle, Lyle took a running jump into the water.

Lyle's water tricks made everyone laugh. Everyone, that is, but Mrs. Hipple who was there with Clover.

Mrs. Hipple set out at once to find a lifeguard.

"Lifeguard! Lifeguard!" she cried. "Are crocodiles allowed to swim here?"

"Of course not," answered the lifeguard.

"Well, there is a crocodile out there, this very minute." Mrs. Hipple showed him where she had seen the crocodile.

Suddenly, everyone was looking at a little girl bobbing about in the water.

"*Clover! Clover!*" cried Mrs. Hipple. "She's going to drown!"

At once the lifeguard pushed off to save her. But Lyle raced to Clover before him.

"There's a crocodile!" someone gasped.

"No, it's Lyle," called Mrs. Primm, standing nearby. "I mean it's Lyle the Crocodile."

Lyle brought a very wet, but happy Clover safely back to shore.

"Oh, Lyle, dear friend," sobbed Mrs. Hipple, "how can I ever thank you enough?"

Everyone was so proud of Lyle. He was made an honorary lifeguard and given a hat and a silver whistle.

"Lyle, you are very brave," said the head lifeguard. "Feel free to come here and save people whenever you want."

The next day a note addressed to Lyle was found under the door of the house on East 88th Street. "Not again!" Mrs. Primm cried. Mr. Primm read the note.

Dear Lyle,

I love you. I love you more than anything. I love you so much I can't stand it.

Your friend for life,
Clover Sue Hipple

P.S. May I play with you today?
P.P.S. My mother said it was all right.

THE SECRET BOX

Joanna Cole

Ann Marie was a city kid. She lived in a housing project in New York. From the kitchen window, she could see ten floors down.

Ann Marie's father and mother worked, so there was always some job for her to do. When she came home from school, she had to clean up the house and watch her two sisters. At dinnertime her mother would say, "Ann Marie, we need some bread from the store," or, "Haven't you set the table yet?"

Ann Marie never seemed to have any time of her own. She hardly ever got to visit Vanessa, her best friend in school. Instead she had to stay with her little sisters. Sometimes they had fun together. But Ann Marie didn't like to be with little kids all the time.

Ann Marie wanted to have something all to herself. So she made a secret box, which she kept under her bed. It was only a small box, but it was big enough to hold a picture of her class, some pretty buttons, and a few other things she liked to collect.

Sometimes when it rained, Ann Marie took out her things and looked at them. She put all the buttons on a string and made a necklace. Or she picked out the kids she liked best in the picture. She made sure her sisters never knew about her box because then it wouldn't be a secret anymore. Ann Marie never told *anyone* about the secret box.

One day Ann Marie was standing near Mr. Freeman's desk. Mr. Freeman was the best teacher she had ever had. Almost everyone in the class liked him.

On Mr. Freeman's desk was a pencil that was red on one end and blue on the other. Ann Marie looked at it for a long time. She looked around the room and saw that no one was looking at her. She picked up the pencil and put it in her pocket. It would be wonderful for the secret box.

The next morning, as she got ready for school, Ann Marie began to wonder if Mr. Freeman knew she had taken the pencil. At breakfast she was very quiet.

"What's the matter, Ann Marie?" her father asked.

"Nothing," she said. But there was something the matter. Ann Marie was afraid that Mr. Freeman would be mad at her.

When she got to school, everything was all right. Mr. Freeman asked her to clean the blackboards, as he always did. She saw another red and blue pencil on his desk. Ann Marie guessed Mr. Freeman had a lot of pencils. "He didn't even notice it was gone," she thought.

On the way to lunch Vanessa said, "This afternoon we're going to gym. Maybe Mrs. Miller will let us be on the same side, Ann Marie."

"Maybe," Ann Marie said. "But I don't think so. She's too mean."

Luis was behind Ann Marie. He always liked to tease her.

"Ann Marie can't even hit a volleyball over the net," he said.

"I can hit it better than you," Ann Marie said.

"Ann Marie, Luis," said Mr. Freeman. "There is no talking in line."

After lunch the class went to gym. Mrs. Miller, the gym teacher, wouldn't let you play if you talked in line. So everyone tried to come in quietly.

Today Luis whispered, *"Ann Marie can't hit a ball,"* and pushed her hard into the kids in front of her.

"You stop it!" Ann Marie said.

Just then Mrs. Miller turned around. *"Ann Marie!"* she shouted. "No gym for you today! Sit on the bench!"

Ann Marie watched Luis playing with a big smile on his face. She felt like crying. She was so mad she didn't watch the game. Instead she looked down at the floor, where all the kids had put their books.

"I wish I never had to see Mrs. Miller's face again," Ann Marie thought. She gave Mrs. Miller a hate look. Then she gave Luis one, too, but he didn't see it.

She looked down and saw a pencil case was next to her foot. Inside the case Ann Marie could see a gold ring with a blue stone. If she had that ring in the secret box, she wouldn't care about Mrs. Miller or Luis or volleyball anymore. Slowly Ann Marie reached down, took the ring out, and put it in her sneaker.

Mrs. Miller blew the whistle. Ann Marie went over and stood by the door while the other kids got their books.

"Don't worry, Ann Marie," Vanessa said. "I bet Luis only acts that way because he likes you."

"I don't care," Ann Marie said. "I hate him."

That night Ann Marie put the ring in her secret box. It looked even better than the red and blue pencil. She put it on her finger and took it off again. It made her feel pretty. Then she heard her sister coming into the room, so she dropped the ring in the box and slid the box under the bed.

"I wonder who the ring belongs to," she thought, as she went to sleep.

The next day Ann Marie got to school just before the bell rang. She took out her homework and handed Vanessa a piece of gum under the desk. Vanessa didn't take it.

"Vanessa," she whispered. "Here's some gum."

"I don't feel like any," Vanessa said.

"What's the matter?" Ann Marie saw that her friend's eyes were red. "Have you been crying?"

"Someone took my ring."

Ann Marie felt awful.

"I only got it yesterday," Vanessa said, "and today it's gone."

"Maybe you lost it," Ann Marie said.

"No I didn't," Vanessa said, and her face looked hard.

"Maybe it'll turn up," Ann Marie said. Then she was quiet. She knew that she had taken Vanessa's ring.

All day in school Ann Marie felt bad. When three o'clock came, it was raining hard. She walked through the water on the way home and got her shoes wet. All the other kids had umbrellas. Ann Marie felt so bad she didn't even care if she got wet.

After supper, Ann Marie helped in the kitchen. Then she went to bed early. She didn't look in the secret box. She didn't do her homework. She just closed her eyes and tried to forget what she had done.

The next morning she went to school early. She was the first one there. She sat down at her desk and took the ring and the red and blue pencil out of her bag. Slowly she put the ring in Vanessa's desk and the pencil on Mr. Freeman's. Soon the other kids came in.

Ann Marie went to sharpen her pencil. As she passed Luis's desk, she saw a new roll of play money. She stopped and looked at it. "I wonder if it would fit in the secret box," she thought. Then she remembered Vanessa. Luis would miss the money just as much as Vanessa had missed her ring.

So Ann Marie sharpened her pencil and went back to her desk.

"You're here early," Vanessa said.

"I have to finish my homework. I didn't do it last night," Ann Marie said.

Vanessa looked in her desk. "Here's my ring," she cried. "Nobody took it after all."

Ann Marie smiled as Vanessa put on the ring. Ann Marie felt good. Today was gym. No matter what Luis did in line, Ann Marie wouldn't say anything. She would show him she could play volleyball better than anyone in the class.

The Hermit Business

Elizabeth Levy

"Are you going to be scared again this year?" asked Muffy.

"No, this year we're going to do it," said Brenda. She handed the field glasses to Doug. He was just standing there looking at the little island across the bay.

Even without the field glasses you could make out the house where the hermit lived. It was a broken-down shack with boards nailed together every which way. From the roof, an old American flag flew from a funny-looking flagpole.

The island where the hermit lived was about the size of two city blocks. There was only one tree on the island. It was old and weather-beaten. And most of its branches had been broken off in storms. The few that were left had been bent into strange shapes by the wind.

The rest of the island was rock and grass. Nobody lived there but the hermit and his sheep.

There were many stories about the hermit. People said that at night or in storms, he sometimes kept his sheep inside his shack. They said the hermit never took a bath and that his whole house smelled of sheep. Some people said that he was the brother of a President.

Doug, Brenda, and Muffy had heard stories about the hermit all their lives. The island where he lived was very close to the island where they spent their summers.

Once in a while, the hermit rowed over to their island to buy food. No one seemed to know where he got the money, but there was talk of buried treasure.

A lot of people said a lot of things. However, no one but the hermit knew the real story.

This was the third summer the three friends had talked of rowing to the island to find out about the hermit business. The trip took only twenty minutes by row-boat. But something always kept them from going.

Two years ago, when they were eight years old, Doug had not yet learned to swim. Nobody was allowed to take out a boat until he could swim very well.

Last summer, when they were nine and Doug had finally learned to swim, Brenda had broken her leg playing baseball. She made Muffy and Doug promise that they wouldn't visit the hermit without her.

Now, this was the third year. After all their talk, the friends promised themselves that this summer there would be no turning back.

They made their plans. Muffy asked her mother if she would pack them a lunch when they went to see the hermit. Brenda asked her father if they could take the rowboat. They would promise to wear life jackets and to return before dark. Doug made up a speech that would tell the hermit why they had come to visit. He practiced his speech for a week.

"Mr. Hermit," it went, "my name is Doug, and these are my friends Brenda and Muffy. For three summers now we have been planning to pay you a visit. Our school is doing a project on sheep. We wondered if you'd tell us something about your sheep."

It wasn't true, of course. Their teacher had never said a word about a project on sheep.

But Doug was sure that the hermit would never know that. He might even take them around his island to see the sheep and even ask them into his house. Then they could look for signs of buried treasure.

Muffy almost ruined the whole thing. She didn't like to lie. She once had promised her mother that she wouldn't lie.

"You have to lie to a hermit," said Doug. "Everyone knows that."

Muffy finally made up her mind to go along with the plan as long as she didn't have to do any lying herself.

Once Doug knew his speech by heart, they were ready. They had only to wait for a bright sunny day. And when it came, they were off!

Taking turns rowing, the children headed toward the hermit's island. Once Muffy almost dropped the lunch in the water. But aside from that, the trip across the bay was easy and quick. Within twenty minutes, they were at the hermit's shore.

And there, on the shore waiting for them, was—**the hermit!**

"He looks angry,"
said Brenda.

"Let's get out of here!"
whispered Muffy.

"No," said Doug.
"It's too late."

51

Doug opened his mouth to start his speech. But all he could get out was a loud whisper. Then he tried again. But before Doug could say a word, the hermit said, "Hello."

Brenda, Doug, and Muffy just sat there.

"Hello," said the hermit again.

Brenda finally managed to say hello in a very small voice.

"Did you come to visit?" asked the hermit.

"Mr. Hermit," began Doug, who had finally gotten his voice back, "my name is Doug, and these are my friends Brenda and Muffy."

Before Doug could say any more, the hermit said, "My name is Ray. Let me help you get your boat ashore."

The next thing they knew, the hermit was helping them out of the boat. "Would you like to see my sheep?" he asked.

"Yes," said Doug, who had now forgotten the speech he had planned to make.

The hermit took them around the island and showed them his sheep. Each of the sheep had a name.

At lunchtime, the hermit invited them into his house to try some soup he had made. Being polite, the children took a little soup and shared their lunch with him in return. As a matter of fact the soup was very good, so good that Doug and Muffy asked for more.

As for the house, it did smell. And it was very dirty. But nowhere were there any signs of buried treasure.

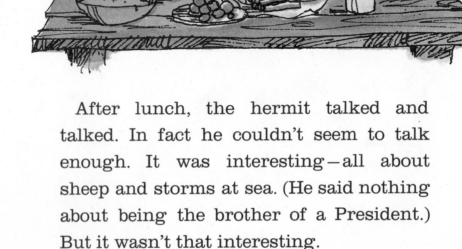

After lunch, the hermit talked and talked. In fact he couldn't seem to talk enough. It was interesting—all about sheep and storms at sea. (He said nothing about being the brother of a President.) But it wasn't that interesting.

Finally, Doug told the hermit that they must leave. "We promised our parents to be home by five," he said.

The hermit looked disappointed. "Well, if you must leave, I'll see you off," he said.

On the way to the boat, Doug was quiet. He was thinking hard. "Mr. Hermit, I mean Ray," he said, "would you like other people to come visit you?"

"Sure," Ray said. "I like to have people visit me."

"Why did you ask him that?" asked Brenda as soon as they had rowed out into the bay. "I don't want to go back there. He talks more than Uncle Harry. And that's a lot."

"I have an idea," said Doug. "You and Muffy meet me on the beach tomorrow morning, and I'll tell you about it."

The next morning on the beach, Doug showed the girls a big sign that he had made the night before.

On it in big letters, they saw:

That summer Doug, Brenda, and Muffy took turns rowing people to the hermit's island. At fifty cents a trip, they made more money than ever before.

The hermit was happy, too. There were lots of people to listen to him. The hermit didn't like to hear other people talk. That's why he became a hermit!

Same Letters - Different Sounds

Read the words in the numbered boxes. Notice the sound for *ea* in each.

1	2	3
dear nearly	east tea	head instead

Now read the words in the boxes below.
Does the *ea* stand for the sound you hear in
the words in box 1, 2, or 3?

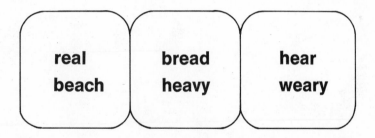

real beach	bread heavy	hear weary

The Haunted Spy

Barbara Ninde Byfield

Part 1

I was a spy who got tired of spying. I was tired of having to wear my trench coat even when it wasn't raining. I was tired of hotels, fast cars, and meals I never had time to finish.

One day I tried to write with my walkie-talkie that looked like a pen. Then I tried to see the time on my tape recorder that looked like a watch.

"Really," I said to myself, "I am getting too old for this spy business. I think I'll give it up and live a quiet life in the country."

So I went off in my fast car, looking for a house in the country.

The sixth house I looked at had all the things I wanted. It was built on an island in a small lake. There was a smaller island nearby with a ruin on it. There was a boat for getting from one island to the other. And best of all, the house had a very fine tower. Really, it wasn't a house at all. It was a small castle.

"I can be very happy here," I said to myself. And so I came to live in the castle.

I packed away the walkie-talkie, the tape recorder, and the trench coat. I traded my fast car for an old station wagon, and my gun for a fishing pole. And with my dog, Zero, I came to live in the castle.

At first there was a lot to do. I had to nail down all the broken floorboards and fix the fireplace so it wouldn't smoke. I oiled and wound the grandfather clock in the hall and shined the suit of armor on the landing. Soon the castle was just as I wanted it.

The summer days were long, and I had time to do all the things I had never had time for when I was spying. I grew some green beans and potatoes in the garden, and I fished in the lake.

One day Zero and I rowed over to the small island to see the ruin. Zero started to bark as soon as we got close to it, and he didn't stop until we were back in the boat and on our way home. I wondered what had made him so upset. Maybe the house was haunted.

Then fall came and one stormy night as I was building a fire, I suddenly had the feeling that I was being watched. Zero barked, and I spun around. But the door was closed, and there was nowhere in the room for anyone to hide. I had just made up my mind that I was being silly, when I noticed my book. It had been closed; I was sure of it. And now it lay open! I looked through the whole castle, room by room, but I found nothing.

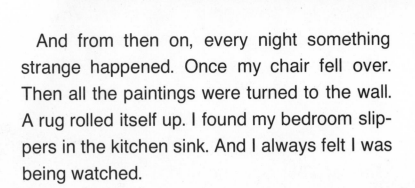

And from then on, every night something strange happened. Once my chair fell over. Then all the paintings were turned to the wall. A rug rolled itself up. I found my bedroom slippers in the kitchen sink. And I always felt I was being watched.

At last one night I heard footsteps in the tower. I jumped up and threw down my book. "I might as well have kept on spying for all the quiet I get in this house. I'll just have to do this one more job and find out what is going on."

So I got out my trench coat, put on my tape-recorder watch, and put my walkie-talkie pen in my pocket. Then I felt ready for business!

Just then, I heard the footsteps again. This time the sound was coming right from under me. Quickly, I got down on my knees with my ear to the floor, and sure enough, I heard the steps. I tore up some of the floorboards, and there was a small stone stairway. Flashlight in hand, I began to climb down the winding stairway with Zero barking behind me.

Soon the stairway stopped winding. I found myself in a tunnel which became so small that I had to get down on my hands and knees. I could still hear the footsteps ahead of me.

Suddenly my flashlight went out. There I was on my hands and knees in a wet, dark tunnel. For the first time I was really afraid. How I wished there were someone at the other end of my walkie-talkie.

I couldn't turn around because the tunnel
was too small. So Zero and I went on for what
seemed like miles and miles with no light and
water dripping on us from all sides.

I suddenly felt sure that the tunnel must lead under the lake to the other island. And so it did. For we suddenly came up and found ourselves inside the ruin.

And there, in the faint, cold light, I could see a large stone casket with a knight in armor lying on the lid. Zero gave a frightened bark as the knight rose up before us. His cold voice floated into the air.

I HAVE BEEN
WAITING FOR YOU!

Part 2

Never, in all my years of spying, had I been more frightened. "You've been waiting for me?" I asked the knight.

"Yes, for you," he said. "Many nights have I come for you to lead you here."

I looked wildly about me, but the door to the tunnel had closed itself. There was no way out.

"Who are you?" I asked.

"I am Sir Roger. I built the castle," the voice answered crossly.

"It's a very nice castle," I said, hoping to sound friendly.

"Be silent!" roared Sir Roger. "You will do as I say and listen to my story. It is a long one, and there is work for you to do when it is ended.

"Once I, like you, wished for a quiet life," he went on. "I, too, was a spy for my King. And I, too, tired of it. I tired of the heavy armor, the hard riding, the wearing of poison rings, the papers hidden in the hollow handle of my silver lance.

"So I came to the island with my small treasure and began to build. But before the work could be finished, I had the bad luck to fall from the tower. And so I died."

"I am so sorry," I said, trying to be polite.

"So am I," said the knight. "I was buried here," he went on. "It is not a bad place. I quite like the sound of the water and the frogs on summer nights. But I cannot rest until my castle is finished. You shall do it for me."

"Is there much to do?" I asked, with a sinking heart at the thought of building more walls and towers.

"Very little," he answered, "for I did not mean it to be a large place. Small but beautiful! All the hard work is done — the Great Hall, a very fine tower, a secret stairway, and one of the best of small dungeons, if I may say so."

'Oh, yes," I said, "a fine dungeon. But can you tell me what there is left to do?"

"There is still no drawbridge!" shouted the knight. "There are no secret towers from which to spy on the enemy. There is no back gate!"

"I have waited years and years for the man who could finish my castle. I have haunted away the other people who lived here. They were not the right kind. But I think you and I will get on quite well. I shall tell you just how I wish the work to be done. The last of my treasure is buried in the dungeon. There should be enough to pay for everything if you are careful. And now you may go."

The tunnel door opened by itself, and Zero and I made our way back to the castle.

The next day I found the chest of gold buried in the dungeon. With it were Sir Roger's lance and poison ring.

And so I called in the builders, and the work began. Every night Sir Roger came over to see how the work was going. If there was something not to his liking, he would wake me and have me make a note of it. Everything had to be put right the very next day.

The new tower was soon finished, as were the back gate and drawbridge. I even had enough gold left to build a small tower on the mainland. Sir Roger was very pleased, though it was not part of his plan, and I used it as a garage for my station wagon.

I put Sir Roger's hollow lance and his poison ring on the bookcase, along with my walkie-talkie and tape recorder. They remind me of my days as a spy.

Now Sir Roger sometimes comes down the main staircase to the Great Hall. We sit in front of the fire and tell each other stories of the dangerous jobs we each went through.

We are happy, but Zero still barks when he hears the footsteps on the stairs.

 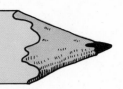

Are You a Good Spy?

Can you decode this message?

2 5   1 20   20 8 5   1 9 18 16 15 18 20
1 20   13 9 4 14 9 7 8 20.   2 18 9 14 7
20 8 5   19 5 3 18 5 20   16 1 16 5 18 19.

Here is the code.

A	B	C	D	E	F
1	2	3	4	5	6

G	H	I	J	K	L
7	8	9	10	11	12

M	N	O	P	Q	R
13	14	15	16	17	18

S	T	U	V	W	X
19	20	21	22	23	24

Y	Z
25	26

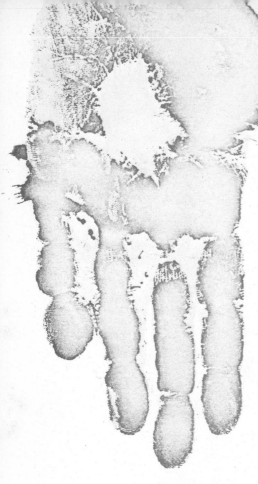

How to Be a Nature Detective

Millicent Selsam

"What happened here?" a detective asks. "Who was here? Where did he go?"

A detective has many ways to find out.

One way is to look for the marks someone or something has made—fingerprints, footprints, the tracks made by car tires.

Sometimes a detective finds a hair or a button. These things are clues. They help a detective answer these questions: What happened? Who was here? Where did he go?

You can be a detective, too, a special kind of detective—a nature detective.

Nature detectives find tracks and clues that answer *these* questions:

What animal walked here?
Where did it go?
What did it do?
What did it eat?

Where does a nature detective look for clues? Almost anywhere — in a backyard, in the woods, in a city park.

You can find tracks in many places — in mud, in snow, in sand, in dust, even on the sidewalk or on the floor.

Wet feet or wet muddy paws can make a track anywhere.

Here is a mystery for a nature detective:

Here is a dish for a cat
and a dish for a dog.

The cat's dish had milk in it.

The dog's dish had meat in it.

Who drank the milk?
Who ate the meat?
Look at the tracks and see.

Look at the tracks that go to the *cat's* dish. They were made by an animal that walks on four feet. And you see claw marks.

A cat has four feet and sharp claws. But so does a dog.

Who went to the cat's dish? We still don't know. Let's look for more clues.

Now look at the other tracks—the tracks that go to the *dog's* dish.

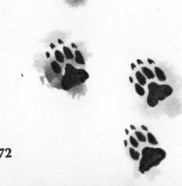

Did you ever watch a cat walk? A cat walks on four feet. But the tracks of his hind feet fall right on top of the tracks of his front feet. So his footprints are one behind the other, in one line.

They look like the footprints of an animal with only two legs.

A cat pulls his claws in when he walks. That is why he does not leave claw marks.

Now do you know who drank the milk?
Who ate the dog food?

Tigers and other big cats make tracks in a line, just like a house cat.

Most of you won't be tracking tigers. But you may see fox tracks.

The footprints of a fox are in one line, like a cat's footprints. But they have claw marks, like a dog's.

What kind of footprints will a rabbit make? You can see that a rabbit has little front paws and big hind feet.

The little front paws will make little paw prints, like this: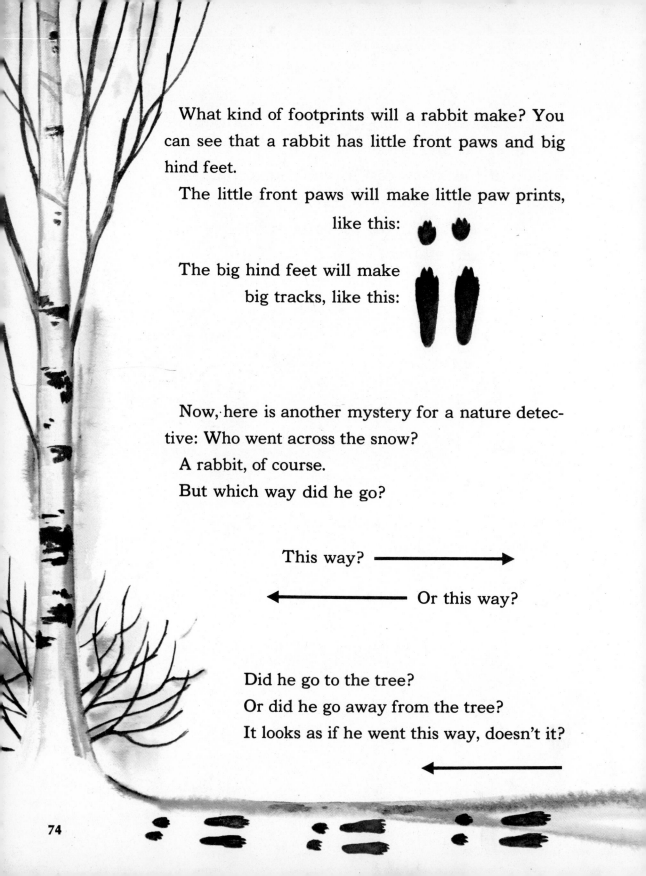

The big hind feet will make big tracks, like this:

Now, here is another mystery for a nature detective: Who went across the snow?

A rabbit, of course.

But which way did he go?

This way? ⟶

⟵ Or this way?

Did he go to the tree?

Or did he go away from the tree?

It looks as if he went this way, doesn't it?

⟵

You can see the marks of the front paws ahead of the big hind feet.

But do you know how a rabbit jumps? Look at that!

When a rabbit jumps, he puts his big hind feet ahead of his front paws.

What happened here on a snowy day?

You can see the rabbit tracks in the snow. You know that they are going this way. ⟶

All at once the rabbit tracks are far apart. That means the rabbit began to take big jumps. He was in a hurry. Why?

Do you see those tracks coming out of the woods? Those footprints have claw marks like a dog's. But they are in one line, like the tracks of a cat.

Who could have made those tracks? There is only one answer . . .

A fox!

Now you know why the rabbit was in a hurry! Did the fox catch the rabbit? Look again.

There are big hoofprints in the mud near the river. And there are little hoofprints, too. Who was here?

It was a mother deer and her baby. They came to the river for water.

Somebody sat down on the muddy bank of the river. Who?

These back footprints were
made by webbed feet.

This is the mark of a round fat belly.

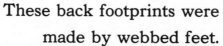

A frog came out of the river. He sat on the muddy bank to rest.

And somebody made these tracks that go right into the water.

Only a snake leaves tracks like this. A snake came down to the river. Then he slid into the water.

Here are more tracks in the mud near the river. And there is a little pile of shells, too. They are crayfish shells.

The tracks look something like the hands and feet of a baby. But look at those long claws! A raccoon made those tracks. Raccoons like to catch crayfish.

So now you know what happened.

A raccoon had dinner here last night. He found crayfish in the river. He ate the crayfish. And he left the shells in a little pile.

What's going on here?

This is what's going on!

A nature detective can find many clues on a sandy beach.

When you walk on the beach in the morning, look for the sea-gull tracks. They can tell you which way the wind was blowing when the sea gulls were there.

Like airplanes, sea gulls take off into the wind. First the gulls must run along the sand to get up speed for a take-off. As they run, their toes dig deeper into the sand.

Here all the sea gull toe tracks are in a line toward the west. So you know that the wind came from the west.

Tracks are good clues for a nature detective. But there are other clues, too.

A nature detective must learn to look and listen — and smell.

He can find clues in a backyard, in the woods, or in a city park.

Who went by?

Who ate here?

Who lives here?

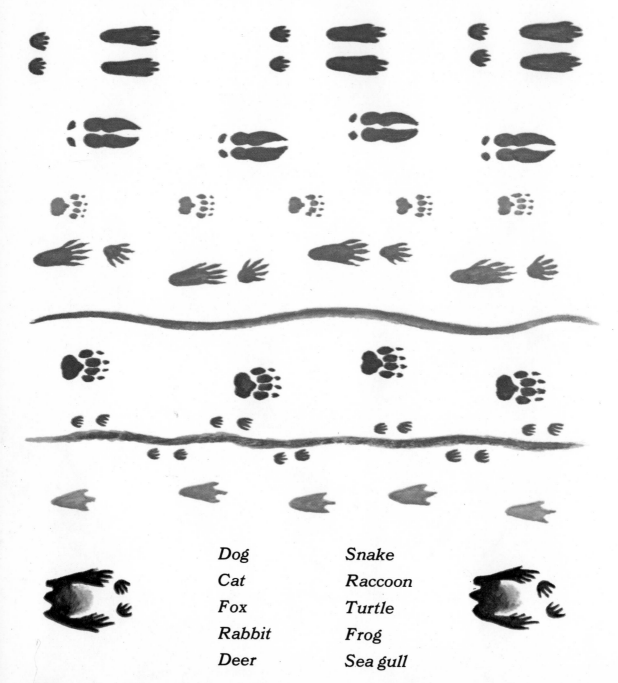

Do you know who made these tracks?

Dog   Snake

Cat   Raccoon

Fox   Turtle

Rabbit   Frog

Deer   Sea gull

Footprints

In summertime
it's hard to know
where dogs
and mice
and rabbits go:
Their grassy footprints
never show—
you can't tell where
they lead.

In wintertime
there's little doubt
where wild and tame ones
run about:
Their snowy footprints
write it out . . .
and I know how to read!

—*Aileen Fisher*

Jill Wants SUNGLASSES

Elizabeth Levy

If there was one thing Jill wanted, it was sunglasses. **Big sunglasses!** No one in Jill's class had sunglasses. Her sister didn't own a pair and neither did her father or mother.

But Jill wanted sunglasses, and she was getting to be something of a pest. It began just before Christmas of last year.

"If anyone wants to know what to give me," Jill said to her mother, "I can tell them."

Her mother just laughed and told Jill that she had already bought her a Christmas gift. Jill didn't get sunglasses for Christmas. She got a model spaceship set instead.

Spring came, and Jill still wanted sunglasses. Her birthday was May 5. She made up her mind to come right out with it.

"Mom," she said, "I want sunglasses."

Her mother gave her a funny look and said, "Birthday gifts are nicer when they're a surprise."

"But Mom," said Jill.

"Never mind," said her mother.

That night Jill's older sister, Laura, talked to Jill alone in their room.

"I wish you'd stop this sunglasses stuff," Laura said. "A joke is a joke. But you've got Mom and Dad really worried. And if you don't stop, everyone will start thinking something is the matter with you. Now I'm your sister, and I know you're a little strange. But I don't want other people to think so."

"I'm not joking, and I don't see anything strange about wanting sunglasses," Jill said. She started to get very red in the face.

"You're blushing," said Laura, who loved to tease her sister.

"I am not," said Jill, who hated to be caught blushing.

"You are, too," said Laura.

"I'm **not!**" shouted Jill, still blushing. And she picked up her pillow and threw it at Laura.

Laura was about to throw it back when the girls' mother came into the room and told them to grow up.

On May 5 Jill had a birthday party. Her friends in the building came with gifts. One friend brought a model of a grocery store, where people used to buy real food long ago.

It was a good party. They were allowed twenty minutes to make noise.

They had plenty of candy and cake cubes to eat.

But there were no sunglasses for Jill.

That night, Jill lay in her bed thinking. She knew that having sunglasses was a silly idea. She didn't need them. Jill thought it was time to forget about sunglasses.

Summer came. Jill's family got to take a trip to the national park.

The trip was very exciting. It was the first time Jill had been out of her building in over a year. First the family took the elevator down 240 floors to the ground. Next they went into the room where they picked up their oxygen masks. Then they went outside.

It was quite a bit darker out there than it was inside the building. Inside, where Jill and her family lived, bright lights were everywhere. Outside there was only a gray light. It was hard to get used to.

Every family in Jill's building took a trip to the national park once a year. The government spent a lot of money keeping the park going. There were maple trees and evergreens, flowers, and even crickets.

Nobody ate food cubes on vacation. The government had real food on hand. If you went fishing and caught any fish, you could cook them yourself.

On the third day of their vacation, Jill's family split up for the afternoon. Jill's mother and Laura took the wild flower field trip. Jill and her father went fishing.

Jill and her father had gone fishing on their vacation last year. They had had a great time. They had been able to talk all by themselves. That was something they did not get to do very much at home.

This year, they had been fishing about an hour and not catching much when Jill's father said, "There's something I've been wanting to ask you."

"What's that?" asked Jill.

"Well, remember all your talk about sunglasses?" asked Jill's dad.

"Sure," said Jill. "I still kind of want them, even if all of you thought I was being silly."

"But that's what I wanted to ask," said her father. "What are sunglasses?"

"You must be joking," said Jill. "I thought you and Mom had them when you were young."

"I've never heard of them," said Jill's father. "That's why we were so worried. We thought you made it up."

"No," said Jill. "Sunglasses are real. I saw a picture of them in an old book. It showed how people lived in the 1970's. There were people at the beach and the sun was out. Most of the people had dark glasses on. The book said they were sunglasses, and that people wore them because the sun was too bright."

1171

SUNFLOWER STATE Nickname of KANSAS.

S

SUN·GLASS *noun* **1** *pl.* Spectacles that protect the eyes from the glare of the sun by their colored lenses. **2** A burning glass; a glass used for concentrating the rays of the sun.

SUN·STONE *noun*
SUN·STROKE *noun* A exposure to the sun coma; insolation.
SUN–UP *noun* Sunris
SUN·WARD (-wurd) *a* wards the sun: also

"Well," said Jill's father. "That really is something. Imagine! The sun was too bright!"

"Sunglasses are great-looking," said Jill, getting excited. "I thought it would be fun to have a pair."

"You know," said Jill's father, "I remember that my grandfather used to talk about bright sunlight when I was a kid. He said the sun was so bright that sometimes you had to blink. I had forgotten all about that."

"Wasn't there any bright sun when you were a kid?" asked Jill.

"No," said Jill's father. "It was brighter than it is now, of course. People talked about cleaning up the air. And we didn't have to wear oxygen masks outside. Still the sun wasn't what you'd call bright even then."

"So you never had sunglasses?" asked Jill.

"Never," said Jill's dad. "Do you still have that book with the picture in it?"

"Sure," said Jill. "It's at home."

"I'd like to see it," said Jill's dad.

When they got back from their vacation, Jill showed her mother and father the book. Jill's father couldn't get over the idea of sunglasses. It seemed so funny to him.

"Say," he said, "let's find out how to make them."

The next day Jill and her father took the elevator to the library and read all about sunglasses. They found out that sunglasses are made of colored glass. Colored glass kept the bright sunlight of long ago from hurting people's eyes. They also found out that sunglasses came in different colors and shapes. People could pick the color and shape they wanted.

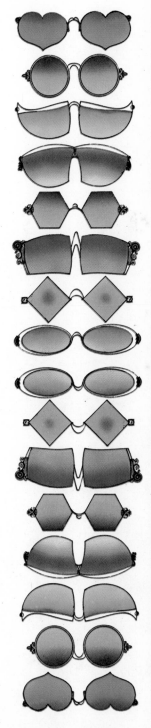

The more they read, the more they wanted sunglasses. But Jill's father had given up the idea of making them. He had a better idea.

"Jill," he said. "Mr. Arnold works at the glass works. He loves colored glass. He's always making things out of it. He's our man. Let's go down the hall to see him."

Jill's father was right. Mr. Arnold not only made the sunglasses for them, he made them in different colors and shapes. He even made a pair for himself.

And when the glasses were ready, Jill and her family put them on, went out into the hall, and walked to the elevator. Everyone they passed stopped to give them a second look. All that week they went around their building wearing sunglasses.

It was fun, but it was only a joke. All their friends thought they were being very silly. In the year 2275, nobody in the world needed sunglasses.

The Rocking-Chair Ghost

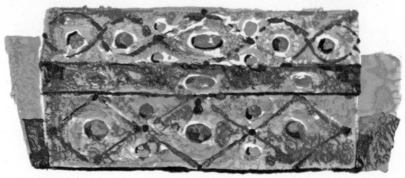

Mary C. Jane

Jody Bright came to stay with his grandma who lived on a street with only three houses. Jody loved his grandma, but he didn't like the neighborhood because there was nobody to play with.

Debbie and Sandra lived in the house on the corner, but they were only girls.

The old house at the end of the street had been empty for years. Debbie and Sandra told Jody there was a ghost in the house

One night Jody asked his grandma about the old house.

"The Cutler house has a sad story, Jody," said Grandma.

"The old house used to be filled with beautiful things, like this little gold box," said Grandma. She reached out and touched her stamp box. It was a small gold box with red and blue and green stones on its cover.

"What happened to the people who lived in the house?" Jody asked.

"Sit down beside me, Jody dear, and I'll tell you about it," said Grandma. "After all, nobody knows the story better than I. The woman who used to live there was my best friend.

"A man named Henry Cutler built that house. He had a store here in town many years ago," Grandma began. "He and his wife had two boys.

"But Mr. Cutler didn't seem to think much about his family. All he cared about was making money. He made the boys work in the store after school every day and all day Saturday. He was always yelling at them, and sometimes he beat them."

"What was their mother like?" Jody asked. "Couldn't she make the father be good to the boys?"

"She tried, poor thing," said Grandma. "But Mr. Cutler was a very hard man. As soon as the boys were old enough, they ran away. They didn't even write letters to their mother. I guess they were afraid their father might find out where they were.

"It broke Mrs. Cutler's heart. She used to sit in the bay window every afternoon and wait for her boys to return."

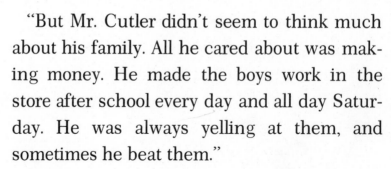

"Didn't the boys *ever* come home?" Jody asked.

"No. Not even after their father died," said Grandma. "Mrs. Cutler lived alone after that. She would sit by the window in her rocking chair and think about her lost children.

"People say you can still hear her old chair rocking and squeaking, if you listen outside that bay window," said Grandma.

Jody could hardly get to sleep that night. He kept thinking about the rocking chair and the squeaking. What could make it rock when nobody was in it?

The next afternoon Jody went to the old house. As he was looking up at the broken window in the tower, Lennie Littlefield came by. Lennie was a year older than Jody, but Jody knew him from school.

Lennie wasn't scared of the old house at all. "I've gone past that bay window lots of times, and I never heard any old Rocking-Chair Ghost," Lennie said.

Jody looked up at the tower again and shouted, "Lennie, look! There's someone up in the tower!"

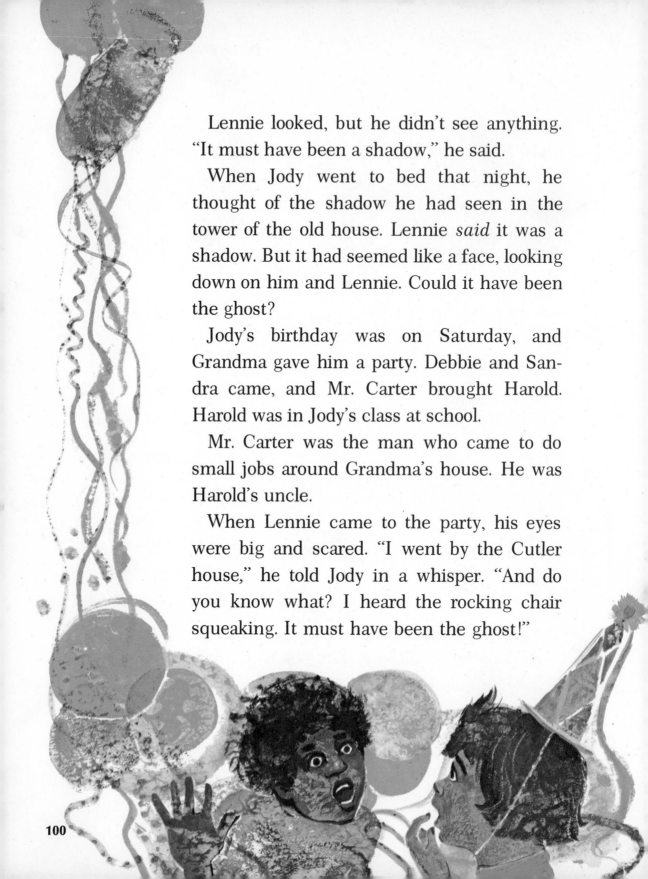

Lennie looked, but he didn't see anything. "It must have been a shadow," he said.

When Jody went to bed that night, he thought of the shadow he had seen in the tower of the old house. Lennie *said* it was a shadow. But it had seemed like a face, looking down on him and Lennie. Could it have been the ghost?

Jody's birthday was on Saturday, and Grandma gave him a party. Debbie and Sandra came, and Mr. Carter brought Harold. Harold was in Jody's class at school.

Mr. Carter was the man who came to do small jobs around Grandma's house. He was Harold's uncle.

When Lennie came to the party, his eyes were big and scared. "I went by the Cutler house," he told Jody in a whisper. "And do you know what? I heard the rocking chair squeaking. It must have been the ghost!"

Jody had to play games and help his friends have a good time at the party. But all the while he was thinking about the Rocking-Chair Ghost. Had Lennie really heard it?

When the party was over, Grandma sat down to write a letter to Jody's parents.

"Will you get me a stamp from my stamp box, Jody?" Grandma asked.

Jody went to the table where the gold box was, but it wasn't there. Jody and Grandma hunted everywhere, but they couldn't find the stamp box. Grandma was very upset about it. The box had been given to her years ago by her friend, Mrs. Cutler.

The next day Lennie came over to play with Jody. As the boys walked toward the woods, Jody told Lennie about the lost stamp box.

"What could have happened to it?" Lennie asked.

"I don't know," Jody said.

As Jody and Lennie passed the Cutler house, they heard a queer sound.

Squeeeeeeeak...

It was a rocking chair that was squeaking.

"It's the ghost!" yelled Lennie.

The boys ran until they came to Jody's backyard. They sat down on the steps and looked at each other.

"You don't think the *ghost* is the one who stole the stamp box, do you?" asked Lennie.

"Yes, I do," Jody said.

Lennie jumped up. "We shouldn't have run away. I'm going right back to that old house and look in the window to see who is there," he said.

Jody was scared, but he couldn't let Lennie go alone. When the boys got to the bay window, Lennie looked in and whispered, "Your Grandma's stamp box is on the table beside the rocking chair! I'm going to get it!"

"Wait a minute, Lennie," said Jody. "There's something lying in the grass."

Jody picked up an old green billfold and showed it to Lennie. "This belongs to Mr. Carter. I've seen him use it."

There was a card inside the billfold. But the name on the card was not William Carter. The name was *Wilbur Cutler*.

"It's Wilbur Cutler's name, but it's Mr. Carter's billfold," said Jody. "He always puts his money in it when Grandma pays him."

"William Carter and Wilbur Cutler sound almost the same," Lennie said. "I wonder if they *are* the same?"

"Maybe Mr. Carter's real name is Cutler. Maybe this old house belongs to him. Why, he might be one of the boys who ran away!" said Jody.

"What about the stamp box? Was he the one who stole it?" asked Lennie.

"It used to belong in this house," Jody told him. "Mrs. Cutler gave it to Grandma long ago. Maybe Mr. Carter thought it should be put back here."

Just then Mr. Carter came from behind the house. He was very surprised to see the boys. "What are you doing here?" he asked.

"We found this billfold in the grass," said Jody. "Is it yours?"

"Yes, it's mine," said Mr. Carter. "I was looking for it."

"There's a name in it," Lennie told him. "It's Wilbur Cutler. Is that your *real* name?"

"Yes," said Mr. Carter.

Jody could hardly believe his ears. Mr. Carter was one of the Cutler boys who had run away years ago!

"What happened to your brother?" Jody asked.

"He died. Harold was his little boy. My brother's wife died, too. So Harold came to live with me," Mr. Carter told him.

"What about the little gold stamp box?" Jody asked. "Did you take it?"

"Yes," said Mr. Carter. "I saw it when I brought Harold to your party. It was my mother's, and I thought it belonged in this house."

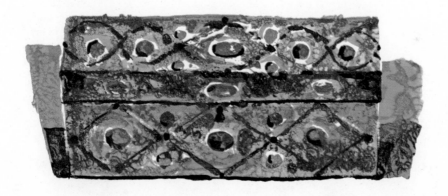

"People thought there was a ghost in the house," Jody said.

"I was the ghost," said Mr. Carter. "I liked to sit in the bay window and rock and think about my mother. I guess the sound of the rocking chair scared people away."

"People would understand why you ran away," said Lennie. "Why don't you tell them who you are? Why don't you live in your own house?"

"Maybe I will," said Mr. Carter. "It *would* be nice to live here with Harold."

After that day, Mr. Carter *did* tell his story. People were happy that Mr. Carter and Harold were going to stay in the big old house.

When Debbie and Sandra heard the story, they could hardly believe it. To think that Jody and Lennie had caught the Rocking-Chair Ghost!

WHO'S THERE?

An empty old house is a spooky place
Where mice run round on the floor.
There's a long white ghost on the
    stairway
And he just might open the door!

There are bats, no doubt, in the attic
And a witch who hides in the gloom;
If she sees you peeping, she'll reach
    right out
And drag you into her room!

But if you bang at the door and shout
(In a very fierce voice) "WHO'S THERE?"
They won't reply, but you'll hear
    them sigh
And they'll VANISH—into the air.

—Norah Smaridge

Stories and Storytellers

Which Is the Way to Somewhere Town?

Which is the way to Somewhere Town?
  Oh, up in the morning early;
Over the tiles and the chimney pots,
  That is the way, quite clearly.

And which is the door to Somewhere Town?
  Oh, up in the morning early;
The round red sun is the door to go through,
  That is the way, quite clearly.

—*Kate Greenaway*

The Mule
Who
Struck
It Rich

Syd Hoff

Not long ago, somewhere in a great desert in the West, there was a miner named O'Hara. Every day he and his mule walked across the burning sand, looking for gold.

"I'll keep on looking until I strike it rich," said O'Hara to himself.

"So will I," said the mule, who could hear almost anything because of his large ears. And he had been with miners long enough to know how to talk.

But by and by the miner tired of walking
across the desert. One night by the campfire,
O'Hara said,

"My legs hurt, my back hurts.
Tomorrow I'm quitting."

"My legs hurt, and my back hurts,
too, but I'm not quitting."

In the morning the mule went on alone.

Other miners and their mules saw him and tried to get him to turn back. "It's no use. There's no gold out there," they said.

But O'Hara's mule kept on going. Even the snakes tried to get him to turn back. "If there's gold out here, we've never seen it," they said.

The mule still didn't want to give up. Wasn't that green grass and a nice body of cool water straight ahead?

But all he found when he got there was more and more miles of desert. The mule kicked his hind legs in anger.

He kicked a big rock by mistake, and a piece broke off.

"Gold..."

cried the mule when he saw it shimmering in the sun.

He started to dance with joy, and the birds flying over could hardly believe their eyes. They had never seen a mule dancing before.

But a mule is not a miner. O'Hara's mule had to hurry back and try to find O'Hara.

He found O'Hara in town.

"We've struck it rich," said the mule in a low voice.

He knew they had to stake a claim before the news got out and there was a gold rush.

They returned to the desert, got a piece of the gold, and came to town to stake a claim.

Now the news was out, and the gold rush was on.

the other miners shouted. And they hurried out of town to stake their own claims.

O'Hara and his mule didn't care. There was enough for everyone. "Good luck," they said.

They put their money in the bank and became very rich.

O'Hara bought himself a twenty-mule team and went off to parts unknown.

The mule bought a large ranch with a ten-bedroom house and a very big swimming pool. He invited other mules who had never known anything but barns to come and visit him.

He gave money to the poor. In fact, he did so much good that the town was renamed Mulesville in his honor. He began to wonder if a mule could become President.

He didn't become President, but he was made a peace officer. He could kick thieves and crooks out of town.

Bad people as well as good came to Mulesville. One day the mule heard the sound of sneaky footsteps in the street. A crook was about to grab a lady's handbag.

"People don't do that here in Mulesville," said the mule. And he kicked the crook out of town.

He kept kicking until horse thieves and other bad men saw that they weren't wanted in Mulesville.

But one peace officer was not enough for the town. Late one night, as the mule was resting his hind legs, thieves broke into the bank and got away with all the money.

The next day the people cried, "Our money is gone! We're ruined!"

The mule went running to the bank to find out what had happened. O'Hara heard the news and came back, too.

"It's true. We're cleaned out. Everybody's broke," said the bank president.

O'Hara didn't know what to do. He had been living way over his head. Now he had lost even the suit off his back.

But his mule knew what to do. "Come, put on your old clothes," he said. "We found gold once. Maybe we can find it again."

They went back to the desert with its miles and miles of burning sand.

Day after day they kept looking for gold. Then once more O'Hara's legs and back gave out, and he said he was quitting. Once more the mule went on alone.

He believed that someday, if he kept kicking enough rocks with his hind legs, he'd strike it rich again.

He was right!

Phillip Viereck

Let Me Tell You About My Dad

I never used to think that my dad was anything special. He was just my dad—the man I lived with. There's only been the two of us since Mother died. And that was when I was very little.

Of course, I've always liked my dad. But he always seemed to be kind of ordinary. He worked in a factory. One evening a week he liked to bowl. On weekends he worked in the yard or did other chores. We never did anything really exciting.

Then one day, Dad got a letter from his old friend, Bill, who lived in Alaska. Dad had met Bill in the army. He had worked with him many years ago. In the letter Bill asked Dad to take a long vacation and come to Alaska. He wanted Dad to help him build a log cabin in the woods for hunters and for people who came there on vacation.

Dad and I talked about it. I said I'd sure like to go. He said that maybe we could.

"Do you know how to build a log cabin?" I asked.

"I'm not too bad with an ax," he answered.

I didn't know that he'd ever had an ax in his hands. He'd never talked about it.

The next day at the factory, Dad asked for extra vacation time. He got it, without pay, of course. And on the very afternoon that school was out, we started for Alaska.

Heading north toward Canada, we drove through many miles of flat farmland. Then we came to mountains that were high on the sides and flat on top. I'd never seen mountains like them. We bought our meals in towns along the way. At night we stopped to camp wherever we could find a place by the side of the road.

One day we came to a place where two cars had crashed into each other. People were crying and shouting. Dad stopped to see if anyone was hurt.

There was a man with a broken leg that nobody was doing anything about. Dad made a splint for it.

When we drove away, I said, "You were the only one who knew what to do, Dad."

"I am sure that some of those people knew how to splint a broken leg," he said. "They were just too excited to be of any help."

Our first few days in Canada, we drove through more flat farmland—almost all of it planted in wheat. Then we came to a land of thick forests and big rivers. The towns got farther and farther apart. Finally the last one of any size was behind us. Ahead were 1500 miles of wild country.

The wild country of Canada was beautiful. The road wound up and around steep mountains. There were forests, lakes, and rivers. We cooked our own meals. Sometimes we went fishing, and Dad cooked the fish over a campfire.

At last we got to Fairbanks, Alaska, where Bill lived. There were wide streets and lots of stores and hotels. I was surprised to find such a big city so far north.

Bill was sure glad to see us. His wife, Ellen, cooked us a big meal. It was great after so much of our own cooking.

We spent the next two days getting food, tools, and supplies into a wagon. Bill had a bulldozer that would be able to pull the wagon into places where no truck could go.

Finally we were ready to go. It was some job getting the supplies over hills, through woods, and across streams. We followed a trail that Bill had already marked with flags or by cuts in trees.

Dad drove the bulldozer. Most of the time Bill and I walked because riding in the wagon was so bumpy.

I was surprised that my dad knew how to drive a bulldozer. Bill told me that he had been the best bulldozer driver in the army. He sure drove it into places I thought he'd never get out of.

It doesn't get dark early that far north, so we kept going until late. It was ten o' clock when we got to Mirror Lake, where we were going to build the cabin. We were so tired, we just got into our sleeping bags, clothes and all, and fell asleep.

The next morning when I got up, I saw how beautiful Mirror Lake was. All around it were tall dark evergreens, that you could see in the clear quiet water of the lake. Now and then there was a little wave in the lake, which I guessed had been made by a beaver.

Suddenly, I heard the far-off sound of an airplane. It was Ellen bringing us more supplies.

The four of us worked hard those next few days. We put up tents to live in while we were building the cabin. With the bulldozer, Dad cleared a place for the cabin. He and I brought rocks from the bed of a nearby stream. We used them to build the foundation. Bill cut logs while Ellen, Dad, and I built the foundation.

After we had finished the foundation, Ellen and I peeled the bark off the logs. The men helped us the first thing in the morning and the last thing at night.

One morning Bill flew to Fairbanks for supplies. Dad took his gun and left camp. He had seen bear tracks and thought he could get us some meat.

An hour later we heard a shot somewhere on the other side of the lake. Soon Dad came out of the woods and said he'd shot a bear. He and I untied the airplane dock and rowed it across the lake to get the bear.

It was a black bear. Dad acted as if he shot a bear every day.

"Your dad always was the best bear hunter in the North," Bill told me when he flew in with supplies.

We started putting up the cabin the next day. I was surprised that Dad knew how to do everything. He gave all the orders. And he was sure good with an ax.

"Best man in the West when it comes to using an ax," Bill told me.

The cabin went up fast. In a few days we had the walls done and were working on the roof. We cut out windows and a door.

At last the big cabin was really something to be proud of. It had big windows on the side that overlooked the lake. There were two big rooms downstairs and some bedrooms upstairs.

By then it was getting dark earlier. The air was cool, and some of the leaves had started to turn yellow and red. We knew it was time for us to go, but we didn't want to.

"Why don't you stay?" Bill asked. "We can run the business together."

Dad shook his head. "It sounds like fun," he said. "But we could only work part of the year. There's just enough business for the two of you. Besides the boy has to go to school. Maybe we can come back again."

Dad sold his car in Fairbanks, and he and I flew home in a jet. I hated to see him shave off his beard because without it he looked just like an ordinary man. But I knew that he was no ordinary man.

I guess lots of people may be like my dad. You think there's nothing special about them. Then you find out that they can do all kinds of things you didn't know about.

That summer in Alaska, I learned a lot about my dad. I learned that he was special.

The Emperor's New Clothes

Hans Christian Andersen

Many years ago there lived an Emperor. He liked new clothes so much that he spent all his time and all his money in order to be well dressed.

He did not care about his soldiers or his people. He only left his castle to show off his beautiful new clothes. He had a different suit for every hour of the day.

One day two men came to the court. They called themselves weavers, but they were in fact clever crooks. They pretended that they knew how to weave cloth of the most beautiful colors and patterns. They said the clothes woven from this magic cloth would be invisible to anyone who was unfit for the office he held.

"These must be splendid clothes!" thought the Emperor. "If I had a suit made of this magic cloth, I could find out at once which men in my kingdom are not good enough for the offices they hold. And I should be able to tell who are wise and who are foolish. This cloth must be woven for me right away."

The king ordered that the weavers should be given some gold in order that they might begin their work at once.

So the two men set up two looms and pretended to be working very hard, though they really did nothing at all. They asked for the most beautiful silk and the best gold thread. This they kept for themselves. And then they went on with their work at the empty looms until far into the night.

After some time had passed, the Emperor said to himself, "I should like to know how the weavers are getting along with my cloth. I am a little bit worried about going myself to look at the cloth because they said it would be invisible to a fool or a man unfit for his office. I am sure that I am quite safe, but all the same I think it best to send someone else first."

All the people in the kingdom had heard of the magic cloth. They couldn't wait to learn how wise or foolish their friends and neighbors might be.

"I will send my old Minister to see how the weavers are getting on with my cloth," said the Emperor. "He will be the best one to see how the cloth looks, for he is a wise man. No one can be more fit for his office than he is."

So the old Minister went into the hall where the weavers were working at the empty looms.

"What is this?" thought the old man, opening his eyes very wide. "I cannot see any thread on the looms, and I don't see any cloth woven!"

However, he did not speak his thoughts out loud. The men who were pretending to weave asked him to come closer. They pointed to the empty looms and asked him if he liked the design and the colors.

The poor old Minister could not see anything on the looms because there was nothing there. But, of course, he did not know this. He thought only that he must be a foolish man or unfit for the office of Minister.

"Dear me," he said to himself, "I must never tell anyone that I could not see the cloth."

"Well, Minister," said one of the weavers, still pretending to work, "does the cloth please you?"

"Oh! It is most beautiful!" said the Minister quickly. **"The pattern and the colors! I will tell the Emperor how wonderful I think they are."**

The Emperor was pleased by what the Minister told him about the cloth. Soon after, he sent an officer of his court to find out how soon the cloth would be ready.

It was, of course, just the same with the officer as it had been with the Minister. He looked at the looms but could see nothing but empty frames.

"Doesn't the cloth seem as beautiful to you as it did to the Minister?" asked the men. They pointed to the empty looms and talked of the design and colors that were not there.

"It must be that I am unfit for the office I have," thought the officer. "However, no one will ever know anything about it."

He turned to the weavers and said he was happy with the colors and the patterns. Then he returned to the Emperor and said, "The cloth is magnificent."

The whole city was talking about the splendid cloth which the Emperor had ordered to be woven for so much money.

And now at last the Emperor wished to go himself and see the cloth while it was still on the looms. He took with him a few of the officers of the court.

As soon as the weavers heard the Emperor coming, they pretended to work harder than ever. Though they still did not weave one thread through the empty looms.

"Isn't the cloth magnificent?" said the officer and the Minister. "What a splendid design! And what colors!" At the same time they pointed to the empty frames. They thought that everyone else could see the wonderful work of the weavers even if they could not see it themselves.

"How is this?" said the Emperor to himself. "I can see nothing! Am I unfit to be Emperor? That would be horrible!

"Oh! The cloth is beautiful," he cried out loud. **"I am so happy with it."**

The officers could see no more than the Emperor. But they all shouted, **"Oh, how magnificent!"** They told the Emperor to have new clothes made from this splendid cloth to wear in the great procession that was soon to take place.

The Emperor pretended to share in the pleasure of his officers and gave each of the weavers a medal.

The night before the procession, the two men had their lights burning all night long. They wanted everyone to see how hard they were working to finish the Emperor's new clothes.

At last they cried, "The Emperor's new suit is ready!"

And now the Emperor and all his court came to see the weavers' work.

"If you will take off your clothes, Emperor, we will fit the new suit in front of the mirror," said the weavers.

The Emperor was then undressed, and the weavers pretended to dress him in his new clothes. The Emperor turned from side to side in front of the mirror.

"How splendid the Emperor looks in his new clothes! And how well they fit!" everyone cried out. **"What a design! What colors!"**

"I am quite ready," said the Emperor. "Do my clothes fit well?" he asked, turning himself around again in front of the mirror.

"Oh, yes," cried his officers.

The Emperor walked in the middle of the procession right through the streets of the city. And all the people standing by and those at the windows cried out, "Oh, how beautiful are our Emperor's new clothes!"

In fact, no one would say that he could not see the Emperor's new clothes for fear he would be called unfit for his office.

"But the Emperor has nothing on at all!" said a little child.

"What the child says is true," said the father.

And so it was that what the child said was whispered from one to another. And they all cried out together, "BUT HE HAS NOTHING ON AT ALL!"

The Emperor felt very silly, for he knew that the people were right. But he thought, "The procession has started, and it must go on now!"

So the officers held their heads higher than ever. And they took great trouble to pretend to hold up the coat of the suit which wasn't there at all.

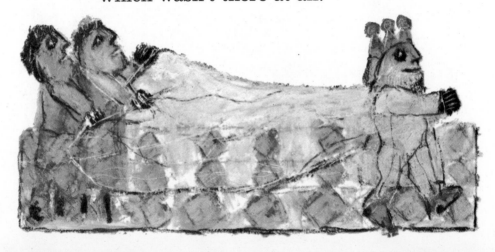

THE ROYAL TAILOR

The tailor who dresses the King
Has bells on his fingers and bells on his toes,
Bells on his ankles and bells up his nose,
Bells on his kneecaps, hanging by string,
So (if you are wanting some clothes)
Why don't you give him a ring?

(He'll always be at home.)

—*Peter Wesley–Smith*

Hans Christian Andersen

Eva Moore

Once upon a time there lived a little boy named Hans Christian Andersen. He was the son of a shoemaker, and he lived in the little town of Odense in Denmark.

Hans's mother and father were very poor, but they did everything they could to make him happy.

Hans's father did not have money to buy toys for his son. So he made the toys himself. The best toy of all was a puppet theater and puppets. Five-year-old Hans never grew tired of watching the puppets.

"When you are bigger," Hans's father told him many times, "you can make up your own plays."

Every day Hans asked his father to put on a puppet play for him. One day his father said, "Hans Christian, I have a better idea. How would you like to come with me to the play-house? You and I will see a real play in a real theater!"

Hans had never seen a real play. "Is it like our plays with the puppets?" he asked.

"Better! Much better!" said the shoemaker. "You will see."

When Hans and his father came near the Odense Playhouse, Hans's father said, "Look, Hans Christian. There is the theater!"

Hans took his father's hand and pulled him to the door. Inside the playhouse, Hans saw rows and rows of chairs. And someone was sitting in every chair. Hans had never seen so many people together in one place.

Just then, the people in the theater stopped talking, and everyone looked at the stage. The lights went out, and Hans Christian Andersen saw a real play for the first time in his life.

When Hans was six years old, he went to school, but he didn't like it very much. He could hardly wait until school was out to go home to his father and the wonderful puppet theater.

But five years later everything changed. Hans's father died. Hans and his mother were alone.

Two years later Hans's mother married again. The family moved into a little house near the river. They were still very poor.

Hans liked to stand in the small garden outside his house and sing. The people who lived nearby would come out to hear him. Sometimes they would ask Hans to come into their homes and sing for them. Hans also acted out little plays that he wrote himself.

To Hans there was nothing more wonderful than singing and acting. He made up his mind to become a famous actor.

No one thought Hans could ever be an actor on the stage. His face was too ugly, and he looked clumsy when he walked. It would be better if he learned a trade, they thought.

"Learn a trade," Hans heard from everyone he knew—all but his friend the Colonel.

"Go to high school," said the Colonel. "Then you will be able to make a good living all your life." But the Colonel knew that high school cost a lot of money. He knew that a poor boy like Hans could not go unless someone had the money to send him.

"I will take you to the Odense castle to see Prince Christian," the Colonel told Hans. "Tell the Prince that you want to go to high school. Maybe he will be able to help you."

The Colonel took Hans to the castle. Hans sang a song for the Prince. Then he acted out part of a play. When he had finished, the Prince said, "Well, Hans Christian Andersen, you know how to sing and act. But tell me, what else do you know? What do you want to do?"

Hans knew he should tell the Prince that he wanted to go to school. But he couldn't say it. He had to say what he really felt.

"I want to be an actor in the theater!" he said.

The Prince was very surprised.

"A boy like you would not have much luck in the theater. You should learn a trade," said the Prince.

But Hans wanted to be an actor. And no one — not even the Prince of Odense — could make him change his mind.

One day some actors from the Royal Theater in the city of Copenhagen came to Odense. Hans made friends with the actors. He told them how much he wanted to become an actor. And so to make him happy, they gave Hans a small part in a play they were putting on. Hans knew then that he must go to Copenhagen and get a job in the Royal Theater if he wanted to become a famous actor.

But Hans's mother did not want to let him go. He was so young. What would happen to him in the big city all alone? At last, she took Hans to the old wise woman in Odense. It was said the old woman could see what was going to happen. Maybe she could see what was going to happen to Hans.

The old woman put some cards on the table. She looked at the row of cards and said to Hans's mother, "Your son will become a great man. The world will love him. One day the town of Odense will pay him a great honor."

Hans's mother believed the wise woman. She would not stop Hans. A few days later, Hans left his home and went to Copenhagen.

Hans Becomes Famous

As soon as Hans got to Copenhagen, he went to the Royal Theater to see the manager. But the manager of the theater had no job for such a strange-looking boy.

"What am I to do now?" Hans thought. "I cannot go back to Odense until I am famous."

Suddenly Hans had an idea. He remembered a famous man he had read about in the newspaper. The man's name was Siboni. He was the head of a big music school in Copenhagen. Maybe Siboni would help him get a job in the Royal Theater.

Hans went to see Siboni and asked to sing for him. At the end of the song, Siboni said to Hans, "I think that you will be a great singer someday."

Siboni and his friends wanted to help Hans. They gave him free singing lessons for a few months. Then Hans's voice changed. The singing lessons stopped.

Hans took acting lessons next. He tried hard, but his teacher was sure Hans would never be able to act in the theater. So Hans stopped taking acting lessons.

After that, Hans took dancing lessons. His teacher could see that Hans loved to dance. But Hans looked so silly. His teacher knew he would never get a job as a dancer.

Almost three years had gone by since Hans came to Copenhagen to become a famous actor. He was not an actor yet. He was not famous. He did not even have a job.

Hans's biggest worry was money. He had to live on the money his friends gave him. He used almost all of it to pay for his little room. He never had enough food to eat. He never had enough warm clothes to wear.

He tried to forget his troubles. He made a puppet theater and put on puppet shows for his friends' children. He told the children stories, too — stories he had heard when he was a child, and stories he made up himself. He was a good storyteller. He pretended he was putting on a play when he told a story. He would act it all out. Even though the story was make-believe, he made it seem real.

When Hans was alone in his room, he liked to read and write. He wrote plays and put them on in his puppet theater.

Hans sent one of his plays to the directors of the Royal Theater. The directors thought the play was good, but not good enough to be put on in the Royal Theater. "You should go back to school and learn more about writing," one director told Hans. "If you are willing, we will send you to high school. We will pay for everything. Do you want to go?"

"Yes," Hans said to the director, "I would like to go to school."

"Maybe I was born to be a famous writer," thought Hans.

Hans stayed in school until he was twenty-three years old. Then he started to write stories and plays.

After four years of writing, Hans was not rich or famous. But he was making enough money to take trips to other countries.

After one of his trips, Hans came back to Copenhagen and wrote a book called *Life in Italy*. It was sold all over the world. Hans was getting to be famous at last!

The next book Hans wrote was called *Fairy Tales Told for Children*. He had always liked to tell stories to children. Now that he was a writer, he would write them.

Some of Hans's friends thought his fairy tales were better than anything else he had written. One friend said, "Your book *Life in Italy* will make you famous, Hans. But your fairy tales will make people remember you forever."

Hans didn't think his fairy tales were as good as his other books, but he liked to write them. He wrote "The Emperor's New Clothes" and many other stories.

By the time Hans was an old man, he was famous all over the world. Everyone loved his stories.

One day the people of Odense had a celebration in honor of Hans Christian Andersen, who had been born in their city. The people in the town wanted to thank him for all the wonderful stories he had given the world.

The celebration lasted a week. The mayor gave a speech about the famous writer. The schools were closed so that the children could join the celebration. And Hans Christian Andersen read one of his stories to the children of Odense at the City Hall.

Hans remembered when he was a child. He remembered the words of the wise woman who had told his mother, "Your son will become a great man. The world will love him. One day the town of Odense will pay him great honor."

Hans's heart was filled with joy. It had all come true.

This statue of Hans Christian Andersen is in Central Park in New York City.

It's a Change!

Suffixes change the meanings of words. Here are three suffixes that mean *one who: -er, -or, -ist.* What happens when you add these suffixes to the words below?

ATU, the Silent One

Frank Jupo

To this day nobody knows where Atu's people came from.

One morning, long ago, they had come out of the desert and had made the African highlands their hunting grounds.

They carried nothing but spears and bows and arrows and a few simple tools. They did not build huts to live in, and they did not till the land to farm.

They called themselves Bushmen.

The Bushmen were always on the move, following wild game. They lived in rocky caves and hunted when they were hungry and needed food.

Living in the highlands was dangerous. Wild animals were never far away from the Bushmen. But at night in their caves they felt safe—safe from wild animals and rain and cold and hot sun.

At night they could rest by the fire, close their eyes, and sleep without being afraid.

Young Atu liked to sit by the fire when he was tired. He was called the Silent One because he could not talk.

Atu had never learned to talk—not the way the others did. But he could talk with his hands.

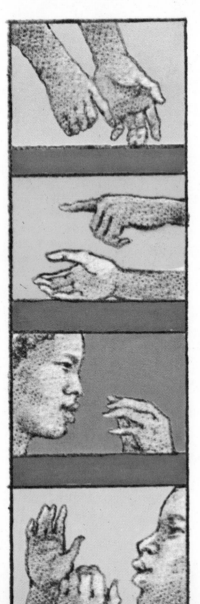

He could do this, and it meant "here."

He could do this, and it meant "there."

If he did this, it meant "hunger."

And if he did this, it meant "thirst."

Atu could say many things in many ways, and his hands hardly ever kept still. He could make his hands talk by making signs. And he could make his hands talk by drawing pictures.

Atu was very good at drawing—drawing things in the sand with his fingers, or on a rock with a piece of burnt firewood.

He could draw trees and birds and animals— all kinds of birds and all kinds of animals.

He could even draw people so that you could guess who they were and what they were doing.

He could draw his mother hunting for honey. He could draw his father making tools.

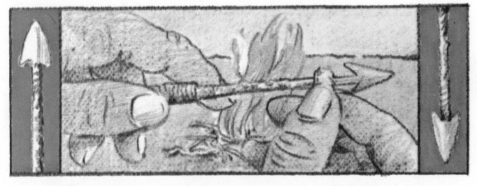

Atu's father was a great hunter, but he was also very good at making tools. From bones and stones and horns and tusks, Atu's father could make a knife or a hammer or a fishhook or an ax.

When the tribe was not hunting, Atu's father sat in front of his cave and worked the long hot day, making the simple tools the people needed.

Sometimes Atu helped him. But most of the time Atu was off and away, playing in the bush or forest.

In the whole wide world there was no place for Atu like the African bush and the forest. There was so much to do. He could take a swim in the water hole, or he could climb trees. He could hide in the grass and watch the wild animals pass nearby on their way to water.

He could follow a giraffe for fun, or keep still and listen as a hungry lion roared far away.

Atu had learned the ways of a hunter. He knew how to move through the bush without being heard or seen. He had learned how to jump and to run. He had learned to find his way through the African bush. He had learned how to throw a spear and how to handle a bow and arrow.

Some of these things Atu learned from playing games. Some he learned listening to the stories told by the brave hunters.

"Someday soon I will be a hunter, too," he thought. "I will be brave and hunt dangerous game, so my people will not have to go hungry. Then I, too, will come home with some exciting story, like my father and the other hunters."

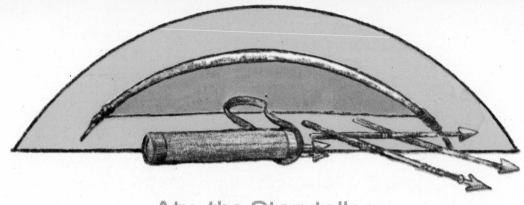

Atu, the Storyteller

One night Atu's people sat around the fire. There was singing and dancing as the headman gave Atu his first man-sized spear and bow and his first poison arrows.

The next morning before the sun was up, Atu's father called him.

"Atu," he said, "the time has come for you to be a hunter."

Atu was on his way with the others. The air was cool, for the sun was still asleep.

The men moved through the bush without a sound, Atu's father in the lead and Atu not far behind. Atu did as the others did as they slipped through the grass across the plain and into the forest.

As the Bushmen stole quietly through the woods, Atu's father suddenly stopped. There in the clearing was the elephant herd—some fanning themselves with their big ears, some just standing in the shade under the trees.

But one old bull had caught the smell of the hunters. He raised his trunk over his head and rushed towards Atu. Then he stopped, turned, and hurried away, trumpeting to warn the others. The whole herd took flight. The frightened elephants tore through the bushes and into the open plain.

That was just where the hunters wanted them.

"That one," shouted Atu's father as he pointed at the big bull.

The hunters raced off, parting the bull from the rest of the herd and running him across the bushland.

Holding tight to their bows and spears, they made two lines, with the bull between them. Then spears and arrows flew through the air at the elephant.

The elephant stopped in his tracks and turned around. Trunk raised in anger, ears turned out, he swung his heavy head from side to side.

At that minute one of the hunters jumped toward the elephant and drove his spear right behind his ear. The elephant turned as if to charge. Then he crashed to the ground.
He lay still.

"The big one is dead!" shouted the hunters. Singing and laughing, the men danced around the dead giant. And Atu joined in.

There was great joy when the hunters returned.

"Well done," called the headman. All the people hurried off to collect their part of the kill and then to have a feast.

After the feast, old and young sat together at the meeting place to hear the hunters tell their story.

"There was this great beast," began one hunter. ". . . so I threw my spear," another went on.

Only Atu, the Silent One, was not there to listen. His father and the headman went to look for him. They could hardly believe what they saw when they found him, high up on the side of a hill.

There, drawn on a rock, the hunt had come to life! Atu, too, had told his story.

There were the hunters starting out with their spears and bows. There was Atu himself, following his father. There were the elephants, swinging their trunks and fanning with their ears. There was the great bull elephant, roaring his rage. And there was Atu's father, ready for the kill.

"The Silent One has made it so the rock can talk," whispered the headman.

And all through the night Atu's people came in the moonlight to see this new wonder. A story to look at! A story told without words!

As the years passed, Atu became a great hunter like his father and the storyteller of his people.

He told of their world, of the deeds of their hunters, of their games, music-making, and dancing.

He learned to make paint for his pictures from bits of colored earth, and he showed others how to do it, too.

There are some who may say there never really was a boy called Atu, the Silent One. We will never know.

The pictures drawn by the Bushmen have been weathered by the sun and wind and rain. But they can still be seen on the rocks high up near the African desert.

Of Atu's people only a few small tribes are left. But they still hunt on the African plains as of old—the last Bushmen.

Talking Without Words

We often tell each other things without using
words. We use our hands, our faces, our whole bodies.
Look at the pictures below. In which picture is
someone saying without words the following:

I love you.
Come here.
I'm mad.
Be quiet.
I'm sleepy.
Hello.

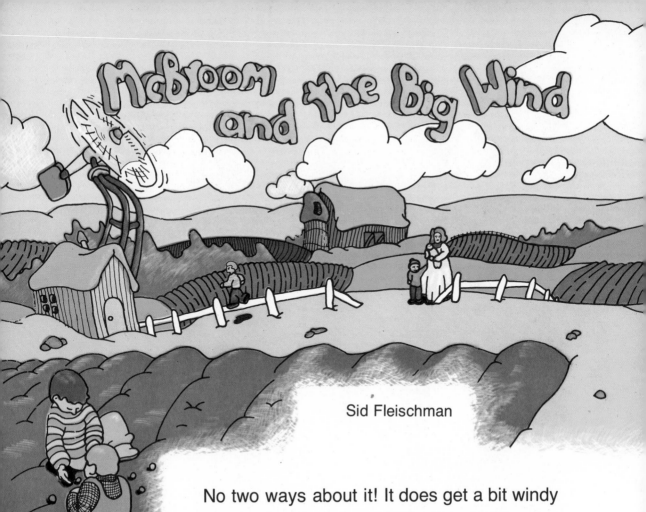

McBroom and the Big Wind

Sid Fleischman

No two ways about it! It does get a bit windy out here on the prairie. Why, just last year a blow came ripping across our farm and carried off a pail of milk. The next day it came back for the cow.

But that was just a little prairie breeze. It wasn't the big wind I want to tell you about. But I think I'd best start with some smaller weather and work up to the all mighty big wind that broke my leg.

I remember clearly the first prairie wind that came ripping along after we had bought our

wonderful little farm. My, that land is rich. Best topsoil in the country. There isn't a thing that won't grow in our rich topsoil and fast as lightning.

One morning we were going to shingle the roof. But the nails were a bit short. Well, we buried those nails in that wonderful topsoil. And in less than five minutes they had grown to just the right size.

Well, there we were, my older boys and me, hammering up on the roof. The younger boys were shooting marbles all over the farm, and the girls were jumping rope.

I had just hammered down the last shingle when I felt a cool breeze on the back of my neck. A minute later, Polly shouted up to me.

"Pa," she said, "do rabbits have wings?"

I laughed. "No, Polly."

"Then how come rabbits are flying over the house?"

I looked up, and there they were—*rabbits flying across the sky!* I knew then we were in for a little blow.

"Will*jill*hester*chester*peter*polly* tim*tom* mary-*larry* and little *Clarinda!* Into the house!" I shouted. "Move!"

The clothesline was already beginning to spin around like a jump rope. My dear wife, who had just baked a heap of biscuits, threw open the door. In we rushed, and not a minute too soon. The wind was snapping at our heels like a pack of wild dogs.

We slammed the door in its teeth. Now, the wind didn't take that lying down. It hammered at the door while all of us pushed to hold the door closed. My, it was a battle! The house shook!

"Push, my lambs," I yelled. "Push!"

When the wind saw there was no getting past us, it sneaked around the house to the back door. However, our oldest boy, Will, was ahead of it. He piled Mama's heap of biscuits against the back door. My dear wife is a wonderful cook, but her biscuits are mighty heavy. They made a splendid door stop.

But what worried me most was our topsoil. The wind was likely to make off with it.

"Push, my lambs! Push!" I shouted.

Finally, the wind gave up beating its fool head against the door. Angry and roaring, it turned and disappeared as fast as lightning.

We all took a deep breath, and I opened the door a crack. "Will *jill* hester*chester*peter*polly*-tim*tom*mary*larry* and little *Clarinda*! Look, my lambs! Look!"

Our topsoil was still there—every bit. Those boys had left their marbles all over, and the marbles had grown into giant rocks. There they sat, holding down our topsoil.

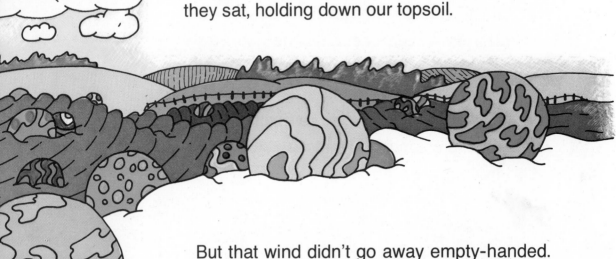

But that wind didn't go away empty-handed. It ripped off our new shingle roof, and it pulled out the nails. We found later that the wind had shingled every rabbit hole for miles.

After we had rolled those giant marbles down the hill, I said, "When the next breeze comes along, we'll be ready for it. We'll put it to work. I'm going to make a wind plow."

I made a wind plow, using a sheet as a sail. After that, every time a breeze came up, I'd plow the farm. My son Chester once plowed the whole farm in three minutes.

It got so that we were glad to see a blow come along. I made the boys and girls some wind shoes out of heavy iron pans. Out in the breeze they felt light as feathers. The girls would jump rope with the clothesline. The wind spun the rope, of course.

Sometimes my boys and girls put on their heavy wind shoes and went outside to bottle winter wind for summer. Then, come summer, when there wasn't a breath of air, we'd open a bottle of winter wind and have a cool breeze.

By the time the boys and I had shingled the roof again, we thought we were ready for any prairie breeze. Then came the big wind.

The Big Wind

It started out gently enough. There were a few rabbits flying through the air. Nothing out of the ordinary.

My boys had gone outside to bottle air. My girls were jumping the clothesline. Mama had just baked biscuits. My, they did smell good! I ate about twenty of them, and that turned out to be a big mistake.

Outside the wind was picking up speed and pulling up fence posts in its path.

"Will *jill* hester *chester* peter *polly* tim *tom* mary-*larry* and little *Clarinda*!" I shouted. "Inside, my lambs. That wind is getting mean!"

In they came, and not a minute too soon. The clothesline began to spin around so fast that it seemed to disappear. Then we saw a hen house flying through the air with the hens still in it.

The sky was turning dark and mean. The wind came out of the far north, howling and shaking the house. We could hear it whistle down the chimney.

Soon we noticed an old hollow log come spinning across the farm, only to split against my chopping stump. Out rolled a black bear, and was he angry! He had been asleep and didn't take kindly to being awakened. He gave out a roar and looked for somebody to chase. When he saw us at the windows, I guess he thought we would do.

Just the sight of him scared the young ones. They sat near the fireplace, holding hands.

I got down my gun and opened a window. That was a mistake! Two things happened at once. The bear was coming on, and in my hurry to get the gun, I forgot to notice which way the wind was blowing.

When I pointed that gun out the window, the wind bent it like a horseshoe. The gun went off, and the shot headed south and brought down some ducks over Mexico.

But that wasn't all. When I threw open the window, such a gust of wind came in that our young ones were pulled right up through the chimney!

"Don't worry!" I said to Mama, who almost fainted. "I'll get them back."

I got a rope and rushed outside. I could see my lambs up in the sky and blowing south. I could also see the bear, and he could see me. He gave a growl. Then he rose up on his hind legs and came toward me with his eyes red as fire.

I ran around behind the clothesline, keeping one eye on the bear and the other on my dear ones.

The bear charged toward me. But the wind was spinning the clothesline so fast he couldn't see it. And he charged right into it. My, didn't that bear jump and jump, faster and faster. He was trapped inside the clothesline and couldn't jump out.

That was such a big wind that I thought I could go flying after the young ones. I began flapping my arms like a bird. But I had eaten too many biscuits. They were heavy as lead, and the wind couldn't lift me off the ground.

I rushed to the barn for the wind plow. The sheet soon filled out with wind, and I shot ahead like lightning.

What a chase that was. If that wind picked up any more speed, it wouldn't have surprised me to see the sun blown off course and set in the south at high noon.

My young ones were still holding hands and just clearing the treetops. But I was catching up with them.

"Be brave, my lambs," I shouted. "Hold tight."

At last I was right under them. But I couldn't stop that wind plow. By the time I jumped off, I had sailed far ahead of my young ones.

I waited. When my dear ones came flying over my head, I threw my rope into the air and they caught it. I had to dig my heels into the ground to hold them. They were too light for the wind. They just hung in the air like balloons on a string. I had to drag them home.

It took most of the day to shoulder my way back through the wind. It was near supper time when we saw our house ahead, and that black bear was still jumping rope.

The young ones had had such a good time flying through the air that they wanted to do it again. Mama put them to bed with their wind shoes on.

The wind blew all night, and the next morning that bear was still jumping rope. He had lost so much weight, he was skin and bones.

About the middle of the next morning, the wind began to die down. We got to feeling sorry for that bear, and finally we got him free from the clothesline. He was so worn out he couldn't even growl. He just headed toward the woods to find another hollow log to sleep in. But he had lost the fine art of walking. We watched him jump, jump, jump until he was out of sight.

That was the howling all mighty big wind that broke my leg. It had not only pulled up fence posts, but the holes as well. It dropped one of those holes right outside the barn door, and I stepped in it.

That's the true story. *Everyone on the prairie knows McBroom would rather have a broken leg than tell a lie.*

The Wind
Came Running

The Wind came running
over the sand,
it caught and held me
by the hand.

It curled and whirled
and danced with me
down to the edge
of the dashing sea.

We danced together,
the Wind and I,
to the cry of a gull
and a wild sea cry.

—Ivy O. Eastwick

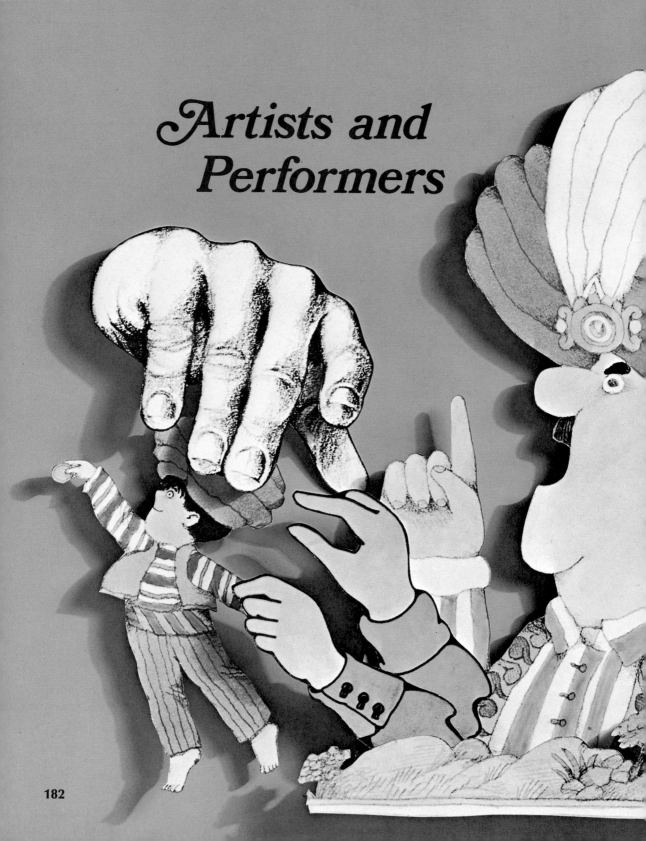

Artists and Performers

If I were a magician
And in a position
To make dolls dance and hop,

I would also be able
To turn from the table
And make the dancers stop.

—*Lene Hille-Brandts*

The Great Houdini

Dina Anastasio

On a bright afternoon in the fall of 1905, a small boat pulled away from New York City and headed toward the ocean.

Harry Houdini, the greatest magician in the world, stood alone at the back of the boat watching the waves roll under it. Houdini loved the sea. And yet he also feared it. Each time he had been dropped into the cold ocean with his hands and feet bound tightly, he had feared the sea. Until he had set himself free and was safely back on board the boat, the sea was a dangerous enemy.

In the front of the boat, newspapermen whispered quietly of the important contest they had come to write about.

"He looks tired," a young man said, looking at Houdini, who stood at the other end of the boat. "Put him next to his young student, and I'd say he looks a little old for such dangerous tricks."

"Boudini just might beat that great teacher of his," someone else said.

But most of the crowd just laughed, for they knew only too well that no one was faster than the Great Houdini.

Toward late afternoon, the small boat came to a full stop. While newspapermen watched, the two magicians were searched to make sure that no keys were hidden on them. No one was surprised when nothing was found on either man. Houdini's hands and feet

were then tightly bound with handcuffs and chains. A rope was tied about his middle, in case the men on board had to pull him from the ocean. Then Houdini was helped to the side of the boat. Boudini followed, his feet and hands bound tightly and his life-line in place. Everyone was ready for the contest to begin.

With shouts of good luck from the people on the boat, Houdini and his student were dropped into the cold ocean. The first

one to free himself would win the contest and be known as the greatest magician in the world. Would it be Houdini or Boudini?

The newspapermen stood along the side of the boat, waiting silently for a sign of life from the water below.

"One minute," someone called. The men searched the waves carefully. But there was no sign of Houdini or his student.

"It looks mighty cold down there," one man said quietly.

"Bet it feels even colder," said another.

"One minute, thirty seconds," a voice shouted from the back of the boat. Still, there was no sign of life from the ocean below.

Then suddenly a man bobbed up from the deep. He waved his hands so that all could see that they were free of handcuffs and chains. It was the Great Houdini!

"Boudini up yet?" he called.

"Not yet," someone answered.

Houdini smiled and ducked back under the water to free his feet from the handcuffs and chains.

Once more, the newspapermen searched the dark ocean for signs of life.

"Where's Boudini?" one of them asked.

"I don't know, but it looks like Houdini has done it again," another man answered.

In a minute Houdini bobbed up again. He was short of breath but still smiling. His feet were free from the handcuffs.

"Is Boudini up yet?" he asked, and was pleased to hear that his student had not yet been seen. Again, Houdini ducked under the water. Now he had only to free his feet from the chains.

When Boudini still failed to come up, the crowd on board the bobbing boat began to worry. They stood silently and searched the dark water for some sign of life. A head was soon seen, but it was Houdini again.

"Is he up yet?" he called. But this time, when someone shouted no, the magician didn't smile. Now he, too, was worried.

Slowly he swam to the boat and pulled himself on board. In one hand he carried his handcuffs and chains. Someone handed him a quilt, and he hugged it about himself and went to the side to wait with the others.

"You'd better pull him out," Houdini said.

Soon Boudini was being lifted gently on board by the rope around his middle. His hands and feet were still in chains. His lips were blue from the cold. He was fighting to get his breath.

When he was able to speak, he looked up at Houdini, who waited beside him, and whispered,

"I swallowed some water."

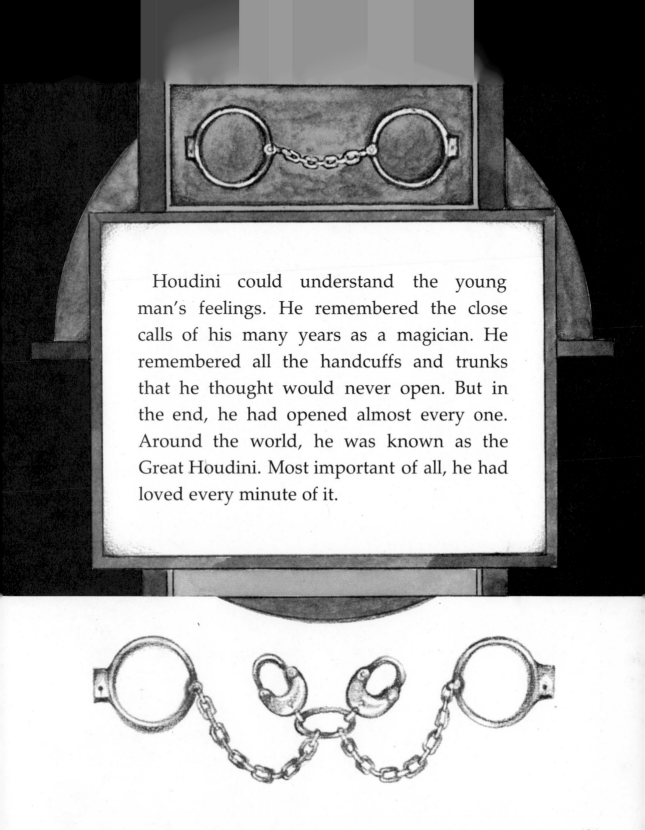

Houdini could understand the young man's feelings. He remembered the close calls of his many years as a magician. He remembered all the handcuffs and trunks that he thought would never open. But in the end, he had opened almost every one. Around the world, he was known as the Great Houdini. Most important of all, he had loved every minute of it.

Stretching Sentences

Read the sentences below. Which one tells the most?

1. My dog eats.
2. My big red Irish setter eats meat.
3. My big red Irish setter, Clancy, eats meat happily.
4. My big red Irish setter, Clancy, eats meat happily every morning.
5. My big red Irish setter, Clancy, eats meat happily every morning on our back steps.

Now you take a turn. Write sentences about a pet you would like to have.

1. First tell what your pet plays.
2. Then add what your pet is.
3. Then add your pet's name.
4. Then add when he plays.
5. Then add where he plays.

Artists and Performers

Egyptian Harpist

ARTIST UNKNOWN

Entertainment and performers have long been favorite subjects among artists. This Egyptian wall painting of a young musician singing for a man and his wife is well over three thousand years old. The young man is playing the harp, our oldest string instrument. The harp was once as popular among singers as is the guitar today.

PHOTOGRAPH, ERICH LESSING, MAGNUM

NATIONAL GALLERY OF ART, WASHINGTON, D.C.   CHESTER DALE COLLECTION

(detail)

Family of Saltimbanques

PABLO PICASSO

Pablo Piscasso has painted many pictures of circus performers. The one on the left shows a circus family between performances. Can you tell what each person does in the circus? Do the performers seem as happy and full of fun as you might expect?

The Actors Iwai Hanshirô IV and Sawamura Sôjûrô III

TORII KIYONAGA

The picture below of the two Japanese actors was printed in color on a woodblock. Notice how the shapes and colors give us a feeling of peace and harmony.

TOKYO NATIONAL MUSEUM

195

Oscar Pettiford

DENNIS STOCK

There are many different kinds of artists. Dennis Stock is a well-known photographer of jazz musicians. Below is his photograph of Oscar Pettiford, a great bass violinist. In it, the musician's sensitive face and hands seem to frame the top part of his instrument.

MAGNUM

Rex Stewart

DENNIS STOCK

Above is a photograph of Rex Stewart, a jazz horn player, by Dennis Stock. By making the horn such an important part of the picture, the photographer gives us the feeling that the man and his horn are one instrument.

Greek Harpist or Singer

ARTIST UNKNOWN

In ancient Greece, as in ancient Egypt, actors and singers played the harp as they spoke or sang their lines. Here is a bronze statue of a Greek musician playing the harp, which the Greeks called a lyre.

IRAKLION ARCHEOLOGICAL MUSEUM, CRETE
PHOTOGRAPH. ERICH LESSING, MAGNUM

THE LOUVRE, PARIS

Performance of "La Contessa dei Numi"

GIOVANNI PAOLO PANNINI

Few entertainments are as colorful and exciting as an opera or ballet staged with beautiful scenery and costumes for an audience, itself beautifully dressed. Pannini caught this spirit in this painting of an opera performance in honor of the birth of a French prince.

The Dancer

EDGAR DEGAS

The French painter Degas is famous for his paintings of ballet dancers on and off stage. His use of color gives us a sense of movement and a feeling of joy.

THE LOUVRE, PARIS (ZIOLO)

Snowing

MARC CHAGALL

In his paintings, Marc Chagall often puts in characters from the folktales he heard in Russia as a boy. This painting has a make-believe quality.

The Acrobats

Flying high on silver bars
Ladies spangled like the sun
Turn just so, and then let go—
and catch one another!
And smile when they come down, and wave,
And are not proud of being brave.

—Dorothy Aldis

Magic Secrets

Rose Wyler and Gerald Ames

Here are some magic tricks for you. Practice the tricks before a mirror to see how they look. All magicians do this. Talk while you do each trick. While you're talking, you can make your friends laugh and make them think what you want them to think. Then you can fool them.

Write Through Your Hand

Say, *"I will write through my hand. First I make a mark here."*

Mark your palm with ink, and close your hand while the ink is wet. Then mark the back of your hand.

Say, *"Mark, go through my hand and make a cross on my palm."*

Open your hand, and there is a cross on the palm of your hand!

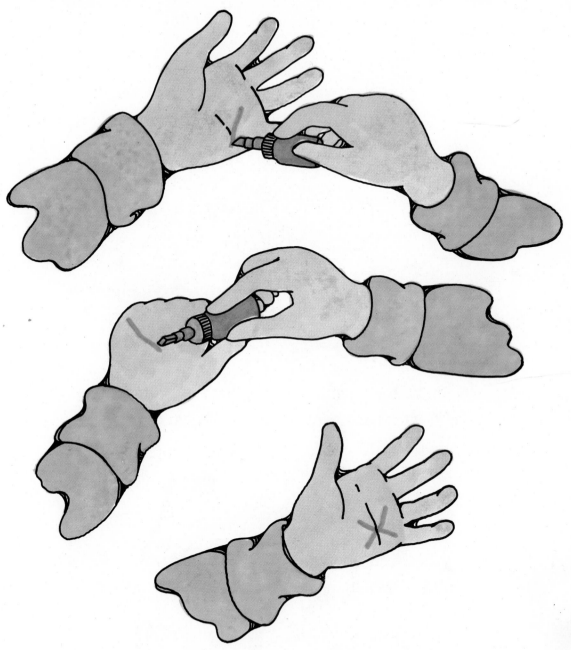

The secret:

If you put the first mark in the right place, it makes a cross when you close your hand.

Good-by, Penny

Say, *"Here is a penny. Watch carefully. I will make it disappear."*

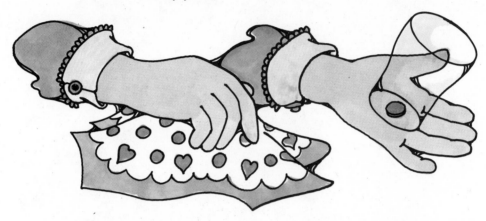

Show the penny in a glass—like this. Then cover the glass with a cloth, and give the glass to a friend. Your friend looks into it. The penny is gone!

The secret:

When you show the penny, it only *seems* to be in the glass. It is really in your hand *under* the glass.

Stick Pins in a Balloon

Show a balloon and say, *"I will stick pins in this balloon, but the balloon will not break."*

You stick one pin into it. Nothing happens. You stick another pin in, and another. Now three pins are in the balloon, but the balloon does not break.

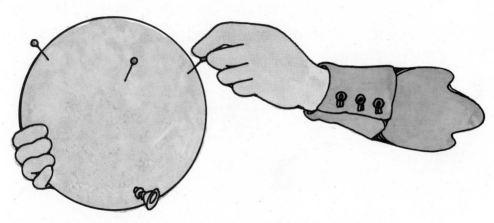

The secret:

Blow up the balloon before you do the trick. Put plastic tape on it. Stick the pins through the tape. The tape holds the balloon together.

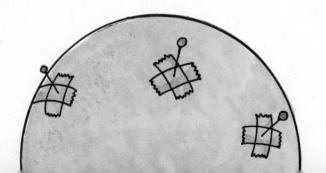

Push a Glass Through a Table

Set a plastic glass on the table. Take a piece of newspaper and press the paper around the glass. Hold up the paper to show the glass is still inside.

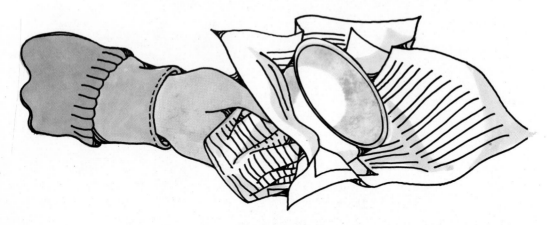

Say, *"I use paper so I won't hurt my hand if the glass breaks. Now I'll put the glass back on the table."*

Then push down on the paper. Push and push until—**bang!** The glass hits the floor. But does it really go through the table?

The secret:

After showing the glass in the paper, let the glass slip into your lap. Only the paper goes on the table. Its shape fools your friends. They think the glass is still under it. As you push down on the paper, let the glass fall from your lap to the floor.

Mystery Marble

Show a marble in your hand. Then cover it with a handkerchief.

Say, *"Feel under the handkerchief. Is the marble still there?"*

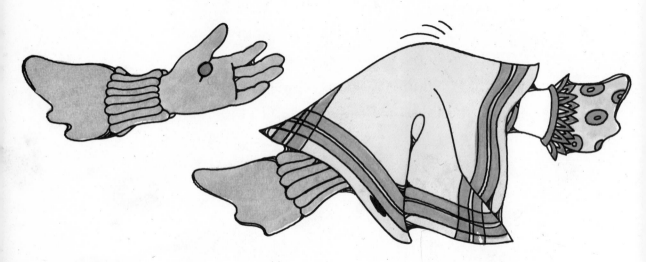

All your friends feel the marble. It is still there. You flick away the handkerchief. *The marble is gone!*

The secret:

The last one to feel the marble is your helper. He takes the marble away.

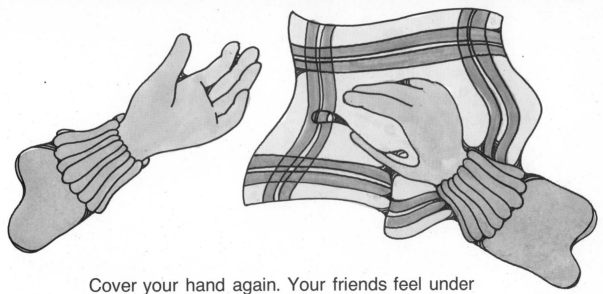

Cover your hand again. Your friends feel under
the handkerchief again. The marble is not there.
When you lift the handkerchief, the marble is back.

The secret:

This time your helper puts it back.

Cut a Lady in Half

Your lady is a paper doll. You can make one yourself. Then take a long envelope and cut off the ends. Put the doll in the envelope so her head and feet stick out.

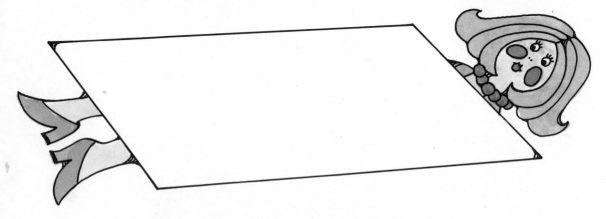

Say, *"I will cut the lady in half."*

You cut through the envelope. Poor lady! But wait. You pull her out, and she is whole!

The secret:

Two slits are cut in the back of the envelope. The doll goes through the slits. Then you can cut the envelope but not the doll.

Don't tell the secrets. Magicians never tell!

HATTIE, the Backstage Bat

Don Freeman

The backstage of a dark, empty theater is a lonely place where only a bat would feel at home. To a little bat named Hattie, this **was** home.

Hattie had lived in the Grand Theater all her life, so she had never seen a green tree or a haunted house. She had never flown in the bright moonlight the way other bats do.

For Hattie, the sky was the space high above the stage. Every night she flew about for hours at a time, sweeping in and out of the rafters and between the stage curtains.

Then, when she was tired, she landed on a rope, folded her wings tightly against her sides, and hung upside down by her claws to sleep.

The only one who knew about Hattie was Mr. Collins. He came in every morning to clean.

There hadn't been a show in the old Grand Theater for quite a long while, but Mr. Collins was never lonely. He had Hattie. Once he made her a little hat out of things he found in an old trunk.

Each noontime Mr. Collins pulled his chair to the middle of the stage and shared his lunch with his friend. He knew that bats like to eat flowers, so he always brought Hattie daisies.

While they ate, Hattie listened as Mr. Collins talked about the wonderful plays that had been given on this very stage.

One afternoon he had very important news to tell Hattie. "Starting today, some actors are coming here to rehearse a new play," he said. "That means you will have to stay out of sight. I don't know why, but people get very frightened when they see a bat flying around."

Then Mr. Collins began to shoo Hattie into the rafters. "I'm sorry to have to do this, my dear," he shouted, "but it's for your own good as well as mine. We want the play to be a success, don't we?"

So Hattie did as she was told. The actors had no idea a bat hung high above them as they sat reading their parts in the play.

Day after day, the actors came in to rehearse their parts until they knew all their lines by heart. Day after day, Hattie kept well out of sight. It was only late at night that Hattie flew down to the stage and ate the food Mr. Collins had left for her.

One morning Hattie heard the sound of hammering. The set for the play was being built on the stage. Hattie saw, for the first time in her life, not only a tree but a three-story house! It was a haunted house. It even had a tower-attic made to order for a bat!

Weeks went by, and finally there was a dress rehearsal. Hattie watched in surprise as an actor, wearing a long black cape and looking like a huge bat, began to climb in and out of the windows of the house.

"Why doesn't he fly the way I do?" she asked herself. "I could show that actor how to act like a bat." But Hattie didn't dare move from the rafters.

Then, at last, it was opening night. Everyone backstage was worried and excited. But because of Hattie, Mr. Collins was more worried than anyone else. Hattie had been very good, but would she still stay out of sight on this, the most important night of all?

People in beautiful evening clothes
entered the theater and took their seats.
Since they had come to see a mystery play,
they were ready to be scared out of their
wits.

The theater lights dimmed, and everyone
was silent. Slowly the curtains opened. The
actor dressed as a bat entered and stole
quietly across the stage.

But the audience had seen plays about
batmen many times before. They were not
excited about seeing another one.

"I wanted to see a **scary** play," said one
lady.

"So did I," whispered another. "Batmen!
That's not exciting!"

But high up in the rafters, Hattie was finding the play very exciting. She loved the blue light that filled the stage. "What a night for a bat like me!" thought Hattie. She could hold herself back no longer!

Down she flew, sweeping through the open attic window, across the beam of the bright spotlight, and above the heads of the audience.

As Hattie began to dart in and out of the beam of light, suddenly the audience saw something that made their hair stand on end.

A huge shadow of a bat fell across the whole stage! Men gasped! Ladies screamed! Eyes popped! Everyone was scared stiff.

What an uproar the audience made when they found out that it was a **real** bat sweeping above their heads. The uproar was too much for Hattie. All at once, in plain sight of everyone, she flew back through the attic window and disappeared backstage.

The audience stood and clapped. **"Bravo, bat!"** they shouted. **"Bravo!"**

Hattie had saved the show. The play was a huge success.

Of course, Hattie was asked to do her flying act each night after that. She was a great star, and as you might have guessed, every night after every show Mr. Collins proudly gave Hattie a white rose.

The Bat

What's that——?
A bat!
And what's a bat?
    And IF a bat
        then
            what's
                he
                    at?
Perhaps he wants a nice fat gnat.
On noiseless wings
see how he swoops
in circles
dives
and loop-the-loops.

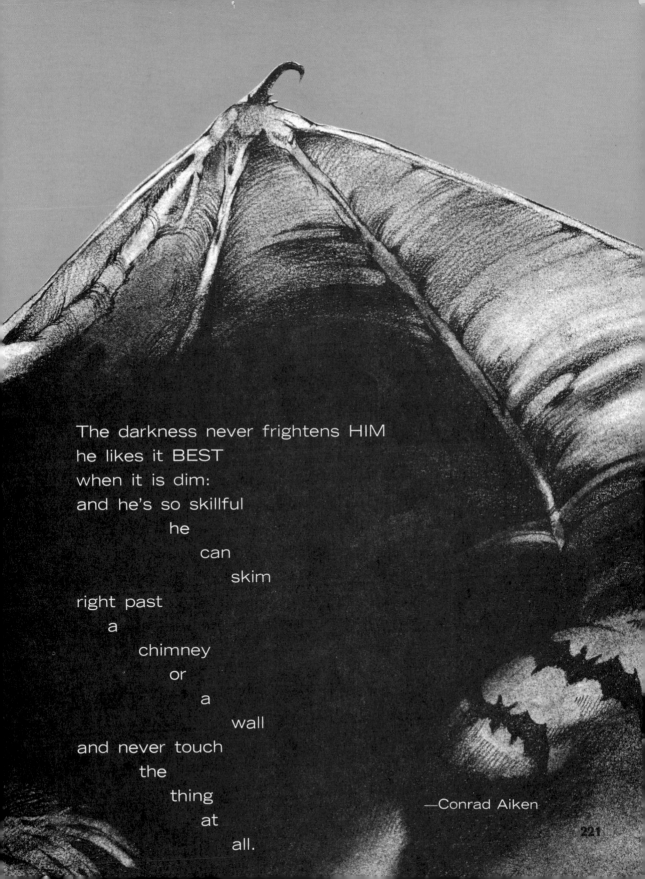

The darkness never frightens HIM
he likes it BEST
when it is dim:
and he's so skillful
      he
          can
               skim
right past
    a
        chimney
          or
            a
               wall
and never touch
      the
        thing
          at
            all.

—Conrad Aiken

The Sheep of the Lal Bagh

David Mark

In a little city in the heart of India, there was a big park called the Lal Bagh.

From miles around, the people, who worked very hard, came to the Lal Bagh to rest and have a good time on holidays. There is a lot of hard work in India, but there are also many holidays.

The people came to see the big white flowers opening and closing in the pond, the orange blossoms on the trees, and the water in the fountain.

But most of all they came to see the lawn mower.

This was not a very new lawn mower. It did not cut the grass very quickly. In fact, it was not a machine at all. It was a sheep. His name was Ramesh.

Every morning, just as the sun came up, Ramesh started at one corner of the lawn. He put his head down and cropped the grass close to the ground.

On some holidays he mowed in large circles that got smaller and smaller until he reached the middle.

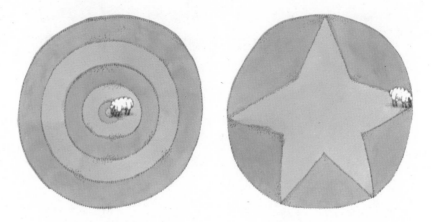

On other holidays he started in the middle and mowed out to the corners and the sides until the lawn was shaped like a star. Ramesh was very proud of his work.

It took Ramesh a long time to mow the lawn on holidays because the men would come over and pat him on the back. The women would come over and rub his head. And the children would come over and get up on his back. As Ramesh took them for a ride around the park, they would laugh and shout, *"Ramesh!"*

Rajendra was one of these men. His wife, Kamala, was one of these women. And their son, Krishna, was one of these children. They had lived on a farm in the country, but they had lost their land and had come to the city. The Lal Bagh reminded them of the country, and Ramesh reminded them of their farm. It seemed to make them all feel better just to say, *"Ramesh!"*

But the mayor of the little town in the heart of India was not happy with his lawn mower. He called the parkmaster.

"We must have a machine to mow the lawn," he said.

"But we can't afford it," said the parkmaster.

"The people want to be proud of their city," cried the mayor. "They will pay for it."

The people did pay for the machine. Rajendra and Kamala and Krishna gave some money, too. They wanted to be proud of the city. They did not understand the machine was going to take Ramesh's place.

The first time Ramesh saw the machine cutting the grass he turned, and with his head down he walked out of the park, up a hill, and out of sight.

He joined a flock of sheep. They did not understand why he ate the grass in circles or star shapes. And they never knew why, every now and then, he raised his head and stood

looking down the hill with big sad eyes. So
they just went on eating the grass and left him
alone.

On the next holiday, Rajendra and Kamala
and Krishna and a lot of other people went to
the Lal Bagh as they always did. They looked
at the flowers in the pond, the orange blossoms
on the trees, and the water in the fountain. But
when they got to the lawn there was only
a machine. No Ramesh!

They could not pat a machine, or rub a machine's head, or climb on a machine's back and
ask it for a ride. So little by little the people
stopped coming to the park. Workdays or holidays, nobody came.

The mayor called in the parkmaster. "Where are the people?" he cried.

"They don't come since Ramesh left," said the parkmaster.

"We must find that sheep!" roared the mayor.

Five men were sent out to find Ramesh. But the men couldn't tell one sheep from another, so they did not find him.

Then Rajendra and Kamala and Krishna went up the hill to look for Ramesh. Rajendra thought he could find Ramesh from the way his body felt, and Kamala thought she could find him by the look in his eyes. So Rajendra started looking at one end of the flock, and Kamala started at the other. But they could not seem to find Ramesh. Then Krishna noticed one sheep off by himself, eating the grass in circles around a small tree.

"*Ramesh!*" he cried as he jumped on Ramesh's back. "*A ride, Ramesh, a ride!*"

And that was how Ramesh came back to the Lal Bagh.

Now the machine mows the lawn straight and fast, only on workdays. Rajendra and Kamala and Krishna and all the other people feel very proud that their park is up-to-date this way. Of course, they don't get a chance to see the machine very much because they are working.

About the only one who sees it is Ramesh. He does not mind now, and he does not hang his head, because on holidays *he* is the lawn mower.

When men like Rajendra don't pat his back, or women like Kamala don't rub his head, Ramesh makes circles in the grass. And when he is not taking children like Krishna for little rides, he eats happy stars in the grass between the water of the fountain and the orange blossoms of the trees.

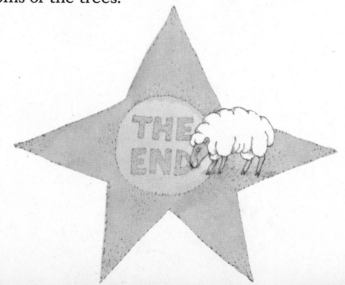

THE END

LiMERICK

A girl on the flying trapeze,
Going through her performance with ease,
    Was suddenly frozen.
    Her partner had chosen
A terrible moment to sneeze.

—Edward S. Mullins

IF YOU LIVED WITH THE CIRCUS

Ann McGovern

The man on the flying trapeze turns somersaults in the air. The beautiful lady leaps easily from horse to horse. The tiger trainer steps out of the tiger cage without a mark on him. A clown falls from a high ladder and gets up laughing.

"It looks so easy," you think.

But if you lived with the circus, you would know that it's not easy. Circus people work hard to make their acts look easy.

Many performers begin to practice when they are very young. And they have to keep practicing all the time.

Circus performers give two or three shows a day, six days a week.

When they aren't working, they are thinking of new ways to make their acts better for the next year. Then they must practice the new acts.

Some people become clowns by going to school. Who are the teachers at the clown school? Other clowns!

For six weeks, five days a week, men and women learn to walk on stilts, to climb up on an elephant, and to put on clown make-up. They also learn all about famous clowns and the acts they do.

There are three kinds of clowns:
　　　　　the whiteface clown,
　　　　　the August clown,
　　　　　and the acrobat clown.

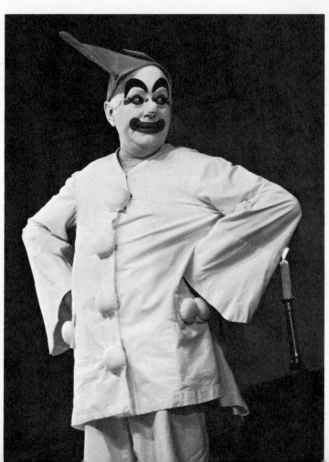

Whiteface clowns look as if they were about to cry. They wear torn clothes, old shoes and hats, and sad, sad faces.

Nothing that the whiteface clown does in his act turns out right. A whiteface clown picks up a chair, and the chair falls to pieces. A spotlight shines on the floor. The whiteface clown tries to sweep the light away, but it keeps moving away from him.

August clowns are funny slapstick clowns. August clowns wear pants that fall down, noses that light up, and large shoes that they trip over.

Acrobat clowns do their funny tricks on tightropes or turn somersaults on the backs of horses.

Circus people call small clowns the "little people." These clowns are the midget clowns who are no higher than four feet.

The tall clowns in the circus are sixteen feet tall. That's almost as tall as three grown-ups. Does that sound impossible? It is.

The tall clowns are ordinary clowns who walk on high stilts. Walking on stilts is dangerous, and it takes a lot of practice. If a clown should start to fall, he cannot jump off his stilts. They are tied to his legs, under his clothes.

If you lived with the circus, you would know how the clowns do all their tricks. Here are two clown tricks.

Tiny car trick: A tiny car drives into the circus ring. Suddenly the door opens, and a clown comes out. And another and another and another — until there may be ten clowns coming out of the car. How can so many clowns fit into such a tiny car? The secret is that the car is empty inside — no engine and no seats. The clowns in the act are good acrobats. They can fold themselves up so they don't take up much space.

Saw-a-clown-in-half trick: A clown begins to saw another clown in half. The saw goes right through the body of the clown. But suddenly the two halves of the body jump up and run out of the ring. The secret? The two halves are really two midget clowns.

If you lived with the circus, you would know that circus acts are more dangerous than they look. If an acrobat on the high trapeze reaches for another acrobat in mid-air and misses by a split second, the acrobat falls.

The safety net below the high wires and bars is safe, but only if you land in it the right way. Every circus performer knows there is only one right way to fall. If an acrobat doesn't fall into the safety net just the right way, he might break some bones.

If you lived with the circus, you would know why the tiger trainer needs a lot of chairs in his act. He teaches his tigers to keep their eyes on his chair. Then if a tiger should attack, it will attack the chair instead of the trainer.

If a tiger gets frightened, the first thing it will do is look for a quiet, dark corner. It will attack only the people who get in its way.

Once a tiger got out of its cage in a circus in New York City. It knocked down a clown and ran toward the lobby. One of the midget clowns thought of all the children standing in the lobby who might get hurt. He bravely jumped in front of the tiger. All he had was a tiny whip which he began waving at the tiger. The tiger was so surprised that it turned around and ran out of the lobby and back into the circus ring. It was captured in a big net and led back to its cage.

Most circus animals don't go far when they run away. One night two circus girls were alone in their tent with their pet dog. The dog suddenly began barking. When the girls looked up to see why the dog was making so much noise, they saw a big brown bear standing at the door of the tent.

The girls grabbed the little dog. They were too frightened to yell. The bear walked all around the tent and then out the door and back to its cage.

If you lived with the circus, you would have lots of surprises!

Circus Talk

"Hey, First-of-May! Tell the butcher in the backyard to stay away from the bulls. We have some cherry pie for him before doors."

Double talk? No, circus talk. The circus world has words all its own. Here are some of them:

First-of-May: Anyone who is new to circus work. It comes from the old days when the circus began its year about the first day of May. New people were hired to set up tents, give water to the elephants, or to work at anything that needed doing.

Butcher: Someone who sells hot dogs and souvenirs to the audience during the show.

Backyard: The place where performers wait before they go into the ring to do their act.

Bull: Any circus elephant, even though most of the elephants are female.

Cherry pie: Extra work. Some people say it was first called "chairy pie." Sometimes performers have to set up extra chairs around the arena for the audience.

Doors!: The cry that tells the circus people that the audience is coming in to take their seats.

Big Top: Where the circus takes place, the circus arena or tent.

Clown stop: A time for the clowns to perform between acts.

Home run: The trip from the place where the last show is given back to the circus headquarters.

Home Sweet Home: The last show of the year.

Joey: What clowns are called—named for Joseph Grimaldi, an actor who joined a circus as a clown about 200 years ago.

Kinker: Any circus performer.

Razorbacks: The men who help set up a circus and take it down again.

Spec: The big parade in the circus in which all performers take part.

Stripes: Tigers.

Walkaround: The parade of all the clowns around the arena.

Web: Long ropes which hang down from the top of the arena. Trapeze performers do tricks on the webs.

Websitters: The men who stand on the ground holding the bottom of the ropes.

Special Happenings

When Something Happy Happens

When something happy happens,
You think of it now and then,
And it's like a lovely present
That you look at over again.

You untie the silky ribbon
And remove the wrapping with care.
Then you reach down deep inside the box
For the thing that is lying there.

And after you've looked and looked
And looked,
Till you no longer feel the yen,
You put it back in its roomy
Box and gently wrap it again.

—*Marci Ridlon*

Kiya the Gull

Fen H. Lasell

Kiya was a free bird. From dawn to sundown he would sweep the sky, the sand, the sea, looking for food. He kept a close eye on the harbor to pick up after fishermen. On the beach he watched the children and ate sandwiches they couldn't finish. Like all sea gulls, he was willing to eat almost anything.

Kiya began the day at dawn. He left the little island where he lived and went right to the harbor. He wanted to be there when the fishermen came in to clean their fish.

This morning no fishermen were in, but the sea had left on the rocky beach a bundle of seaweed, crabs, and snails—all tangled in wire.

Kiya flew around the bundle. When he had found it quite safe, he went to work. He had to pick out the seaweed to reach the snails and crabs. But the wire kept getting in his way.

Kiya had to tug at the wire until one end came free. Then he put his head in the opening and pulled out the seaweed.

Other gulls, hungry for breakfast, joined him. They pulled at the wire and picked out the seaweed. They ate what they could. They flew away with snails in their bills to break the hard shells by dropping them on rocks.

When the party was over, Kiya found that now it was he who was tangled in the wire.

"Kiya-kiya-kiya," he cried.

The harder Kiya tried to free himself, the tighter the wire pulled. At last he freed his wings, but a loop of wire bound his back and one leg so tightly that he could not move it.

A boy was sitting in his boat watching the gulls. When he saw Kiya's trouble, he got out and ran toward the bird. The frightened Kiya flapped his wings and rose out of reach, even though the wire cut into his back and leg.

The bird glided over to the sandy beach and made a clumsy landing on one foot. He hopped along the cool, hard sand near the water, dragging part of the wire that bound him.

People were already gathering on the beach for a day in the sun.

"Look at the sea gull!" someone called. "He's all tangled up in something."

People ran toward Kiya. Hands reached out for him. Beating his wings, Kiya managed to raise himself again.

He flew to the high dune where the sea gulls perch at noon. The other gulls were still away looking for their morning meal. Hungry as Kiya was, it hurt him too much to fly. He wanted only to be left in peace.

Then children came to climb the dune and slide down the warm sand.

"Look!" one cried. "That sea gull is all tangled up. Let's catch him!"

Kiya watched the children come closer and closer. He spread his wings and tried to fly. At last he rose out of their reach.

Kiya landed on the water. The cool waves washed his cuts. He bobbed on the waves and let them draw him out to sea. How was he going to get rid of the wire? How was he going to find something to eat?

Suddenly, there was that boy again, heading toward him in his boat. Kiya tried to swim away. But with only one leg, it was hard to keep from going round and round.

Kiya saw two hands reaching for him. He beat his wings to raise himself away from the hands. Once more he was safe in the air.

Where could he go but back to his island? There were too many people on the mainland forever trying to catch him. In all his life no one had ever tried to catch him. Why now, when he was in pain?

Kiya landed on his perch. At first the other gulls gave him his place on the roof of the old shack. But when they saw his cuts, they no longer wanted him around. He was not one of them. He was tangled and hurt.

A gull flying in pushed him. Then all at once the gulls turned on him and drove him to the ground. Dragging his wire behind, Kiya hopped away and hid in the tall grass.

When evening brought still more gulls, Kiya hopped to the other side of the island. Then as he was trying to get to the top of a sand dune, his wire caught on a bush, and he was held fast.

The sun was low in the West when the boat came in sight, bringing the boy to the island. Kiya watched the boy wade ashore and then turn and walk away from him along the beach.

Kiya was well hidden where he was. If he didn't move, the boy would never find him, and soon it would be dark.

But the boy came back and built a fire on the beach, just below the bush where Kiya was caught. The bird watched the flames until at last he fell asleep.

During the night Kiya woke to find the fire still burning low. At dawn the fire had gone out, but the boy was still asleep in his sleeping bag. Now was the time for Kiya to get away, before the boy woke and found him. He threw his weight against the wire and beat his poor lame wings against the bush. "Kiya-kiya-kiya," he cried.

The uproar woke the boy. He climbed the hill and stood above Kiya. They looked at one another, bird and boy. Kiya knew his time had come. He opened his bill to bite at the reaching hand, but the boy closed it over his head.

"Easy now!" said the boy as he tried to free the bird from the wire.

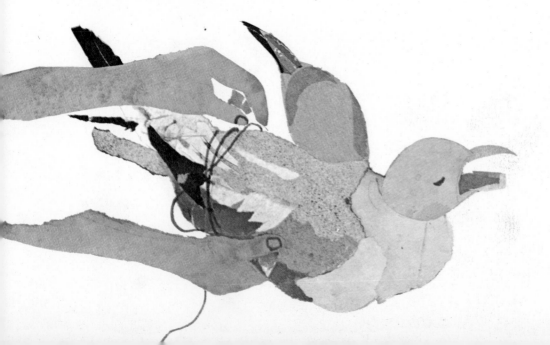

Kiya gave up trying to fight and lay still. At last the boy was able to lift the loop of wire from the bird's back and to wind it off his leg. Then two hands lifted him gently and set him on his feet.

Kiya tried to take a step. He limped, but he could walk. The bird could not believe what had happened. He looked at the boy standing over him. The hands that had freed him from the wire were no longer reaching for him.

The boy asked, "Will you be all right?"

Kiya felt free. When he flapped his wings, there was no cutting wire. Though he was weak, he could fly. Slowly he rose into the air and flew around the boy, who was looking up at him. Then he glided down to the water to bob awhile on the waves. Why had he been so

frightened of the boy with the reaching hands?

   All summer Kiya flew over the harbor and the beach. There were many boys. There were many boats. Was there one there who had freed him from the wire?

   And the boy with the boat looked up and wondered, of all those sea gulls gliding above, was there one he knew? Which was the gull he had saved?

DOES IT FIT?

Read the sentences below. Do they fit the pictures?

Kiya would sweep the sky.

The statue was in the heart of the city.

The bear charged.

Ann Marie was a city kid.

Which word in each sentence has more than one meaning? Do you know other words like that? Use them in sentences. Then draw funny pictures to go with them.

THE SWINGING BRIDGE

Mellicent Humason Lee

It was early dawn in the mountains of Mexico. In an Indian village hidden in the evergreen trees, cold dawn was creeping into a tiny hut. Marcos turned over on his sleeping mat of woven palm. Cold dawn touched his shoulder. He turned over again. Cold dawn met his face. And then he remembered!

This was the day he was going to the great city to find work! This was the day he was going to leave his home.

Now the Indian boy got up stiffly. He moved his legs and arms until they felt easy again. The boy put on his jacket. Then he took his pointed hat from a hook and set it over his thick, black hair. He rolled his sleeping mat and rain cape into a snug bundle for his back.

Now Marcos was ready for the trail. He looked at his sleeping parents and stole out of the hut.

"I will not wake them," he said to himself. "They are tired out from planting the corn yesterday, and they know that I must take the trail at dawn."

Down, down, down the trail he went into the valley, and then up, up, up again. In the late afternoon, the mountainside he was climbing grew steeper and steeper.

He stopped on the mountaintop and looked down. Under his black hat, his dark eyes were wide. His chest rose and fell quickly under his dusty jacket. He was looking into a deep, wide canyon between this mountain and the mountain ahead. Steep, sharp rocks faced each mountain. Far down in the canyon between the mountains ran a river that looked like a thread of blue yarn.

But that was not all. Hung from mountainside to mountainside was a swinging bridge made of vines. It looked as frail as a spider web as it hung there shimmering in the setting sun. In the middle it dipped way down.

How could Marcos have forgotten this swinging bridge? His mother and father had talked about it many times. But somehow it had seemed more like a dream bridge than a real bridge. And now he would have to cross it.

Slowly he wove his way down through the rocks to the swinging bridge of vines. Right across the canyon it hung, quiet now that no footsteps were upon it.

The boy remembered a story his father had told him one day. An old woman of the tribe was afraid to cross the bridge. One of the men used his red sash to blindfold her so that she could not see the water far below. Then she crossed easily. But one man walked before her and one behind.

Marcos closed his eyes. He could feel his heart beating. He could almost hear it beating. He looked back toward the trail over which he had come. Would he have to turn back?

"There is no one to blindfold me with his sash," he thought. "Shall I blindfold myself? That would not be wise, for there is no one to walk before me. No one." Marcos thought a long minute. "Shall I go back?" Then he laughed aloud and faced the bridge again.

"If this bridge holds others, it will hold me. How can I reach the great city unless I cross this bridge? It will always stand between me and the great city."

Now bravely he set one dusty foot on the bridge and took hold of the vine rail with one hand. The bridge swung like a spider web in the wind. He closed his eyes tight. Then he opened them wide again. He took one step, and then another, and then another. Soon he was walking in the very middle of the bridge.

264

He kept his eyes on the mountain before him. "I must not look down!" he thought. But it seemed as if he must look down. A voice in the river seemed to be calling, "Look down! Look down!"

And then Marcos laughed aloud again. **"You can't fool me, old river! I won't look down, but even if I did, you wouldn't make my head spin! This is the bridge of my people and I am at home on it!"**

And so Marcos crossed the bridge made of vines for the first time. And he felt a little ashamed that he had been afraid of such a beautiful thing.

"I have done the hardest thing first," he thought, as he walked up the other mountain. "Now things will not seem so hard in the great city."

BRIDGES

Old London Bridge was very wide
With shops and houses on each side.
And Brooklyn Bridge is very high;
It seems to hang down from the sky.
But, oh, last night, from chair to table,
A spider flung her silver cable
And straight across the air she sped
Upon a bridge as thin as thread.

—Rowena Bennett

Not Enough
Indians

Betty Horvath

Not everybody could belong to the Maple Street Gang. First you had to live on Maple Street. Then you had to be eight years old. And you had to be in the third grade. Those were the rules.

There were six boys in the Maple Street Gang—Peter, Chester, Rich, Ted, Harry and Bobby. And there was Mary Edith.

The gang met every Saturday at Peter Martin's house to elect officers. Everybody got a turn to be president. Everybody was happy. The Maple Street Gang might have gone on like that forever.

Then two things happened, almost at once. The third grade began learning about Indians, and Peter Martin's family got a tent. The tent was set up in the backyard.

"It looks a lot like a wigwam," Peter said. "*A big, green wigwam!*"

And that gave Peter an idea. "Good-by, Maple Street Gang," he said. "Hello, Maple Street Indians!" He could hardly wait for Saturday.

When Saturday came, Mary Edith was late to the meeting. All six of the gang were sitting on the floor of the tent when she came in with refreshments.

"I'm sorry, Mary Edith," said Peter. "You can't belong anymore. We aren't a gang anymore. We're Indians, and we're having a powwow."

"So we're Indians," said Mary Edith.

"Yes, but whoever heard of a *girl* Indian?" said Harry.

"What about Pocahontas?"

"Oh, sure. But whoever heard of girls at powwows? Get lost!" said Harry.

"I *never* get lost," said Mary Edith. "I always know where I'm going. I wouldn't know *how* to get lost."

"Try *that* way," said Bobby, as he pointed up the street.

"Beat it!"

"OK," said Mary Edith. "Have it your way. You think you're smart, but you're making a big mistake. Your tribe will not have a harvest this fall, and you will all be starving this winter."

She took the refreshments and walked out of the tent.

Peter beat on the tom-tom. "The powwow will please come to order! The first thing we have to do is elect a chief."

Peter passed out paper and pencils so the boys could vote in secret. When he collected the votes and counted them, he found that each boy had voted for himself.

"Look, you guys. We can't *all* be chiefs. We'll vote again. Just vote for the brave you think will make the best chief," said Peter.

The boys voted the same way again.

"This is my wigwam," Peter told the boys, "and if I want to be chief, you should elect me."

But the boys didn't like that idea.

"All right," said Peter. "We'll *all* be chiefs. But I don't think it will work."

"I'll be Gray Horse," said Peter.
"I'll be Sitting Bull," said Rich.
"I'm Running Deer," said Ted.
"I'm Red Cloud," said Harry.
"I'm Green Arrow," said Bobby.
"I'm hungry," said Chester.

"That's not even a name," Gray Horse said. "If you want to belong to the Maple Street Indians, you've got to have an Indian name."

"I'm Hungry Dog, then," said Chester. "I wish Mary Edith had left her refreshments."

Without any refreshments, the Maple Street Indians were getting restless. Peter could see it was going to be a very short powwow unless he could think of something to keep them interested.

"How about a ball game?" he said.

The Indians looked at each other and shook their heads. "We can't have a ball game," said Sitting Bull. "Chiefs didn't play baseball in those days."

One by one the Indians left the wigwam and Peter was alone.

"Guess I'll go see what Mary Edith is doing," he said to himself.

Mary Edith was sitting in front of her house when Peter came by.

"Oh, it's you," said Mary Edith looking up from her book. "Why don't you just go away?"

"Oh, Mary Edith," said Peter.

"Beat it," she said.

"Well," said Peter. "I've got a lot to do this afternoon, anyway." And he headed for home.

At home Peter practiced beating on his tom-tom until his mother asked him please to stop for a while. Then he tried to make a bow and arrow, but that didn't work.

"I think I'll go spy out the land," he said.

He walked up the street and saw all the Maple Street Indians in front of Mary Edith's house. Mary Edith was sitting next to an old table filled with strings of beads, mirrors, colored buttons, and refreshments.

"What's going on here?" asked Peter.

"This is a trading post," said Mary Edith.

"How much is that string of red beads?" Peter asked.

"Indians trade furs," said Mary Edith. "Have you got any furs to trade?"

"My mother has a fur piece," said Peter, "but I don't think she'd let me trade it for a string of red beads."

"Too bad," said Mary Edith. "No furs, no beads. I'm not giving these things away."

"Can't we use wampum?" asked Green Arrow.

"Wampum?" said Mary Edith. "Well, maybe. If you mean real wampum money."

"Can we buy now and pay later?" asked Running Deer.

Mary Edith thought about that. Then she shook her head.

The Maple Street Indians ran off to their own wigwams to get their wampum.

Trading was good for a while, and in ten minutes the trading post hadn't a bead or a mirror or a button left. The refreshments were all gone, too, and the Maple Street Indians were broke.

As the Indians walked down the street, Chester said, "It's going to be a long week without spending money."

"No movies and no comics," said Ted.

"No ice cream, no candy," said Rich.

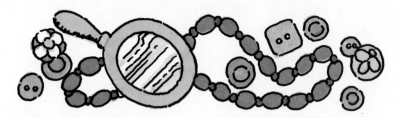

"I don't know why we don't just let Mary Edith be an Indian, anyway," said Chester. "She's not so bad."

Everybody thought that was a good idea.
They all went back to Mary Edith's house.
"Mary Edith," yelled Peter. "You can
join the Maple Street Indians if you want to."

"Is that so?" said Mary Edith. "I'm not so
sure I want to join a tribe of poor Indians.
I'd rather own a trading post and be rich."
"Come on, Mary Edith," said Peter. "You'd
like being an Indian."

"Oh, no!" said Mary Edith. "Not unless I get to go to every powwow."

"All right, all right," said Ted. "You can go to every powwow. But there's one thing you *can't* do. You can't be chief."

"Chief? Who wants to be a chief?" said Mary Edith. "Your trouble is you've got too many chiefs and not enough Indians. And that's no way to run an Indian tribe. You should have an election and elect just one chief."

The seven Maple Street Indians walked back to Peter's wigwam and held another election.

This time there was one vote each for Chester, Rich, Ted, Harry, and Bobby.

And *two* votes for Peter. After that, the seven Maple Street Indians sat on the floor of the wigwam and shared wampum and beads.

Mary Edith found a peppermint stick in her pocket and passed it around. And they all took a piece of the peppermint peace pipe.

Sound of Sunshine,
Sound of Rain

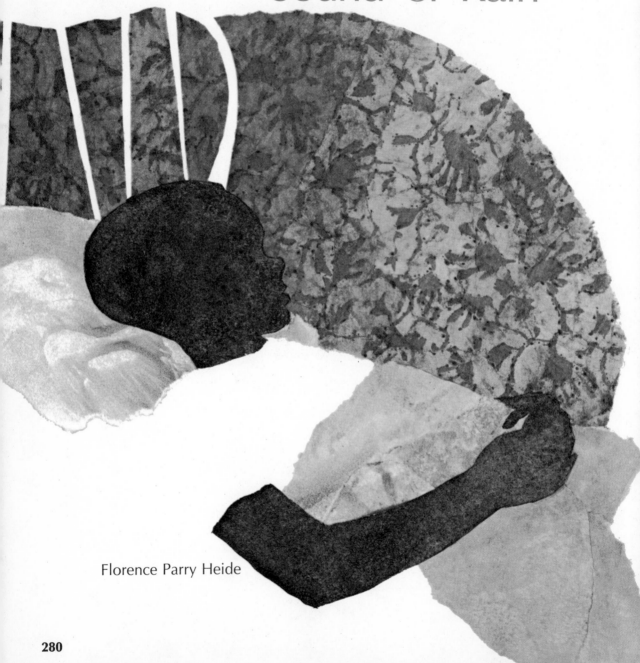

Florence Parry Heide

Part One

It must be morning, for I hear the morning voices.

I have been dreaming of a sound that whispers *Follow me, Follow me*, but not in words. I follow the sound up and up until I feel I am floating in the air.

Now I am awake, and I listen to the voices.

My mother's voice is as warm and soft as a pillow.

My sister's voice is little and sharp and high, like needles flying in the air.

I do not listen to the words but to the sound. Low, high, low, high, soft, hard, soft, hard, and then the sounds coming together at the same time and making a new sound. And with it all, the sharp sounds of my sister's heels putting holes in what I hear.

Then I hear the slamming of kitchen drawers and the banging of pans, and there is no more talking.

My bed is in the living room. I reach out to feel if my mother has put my clothes on the chair beside my bed. They are there, and I feel the smoothness and the roughness of them.

I reach under the chair to find which shoes my mother has put there. They are my outside shoes, not my slippers, so today must be a warm day. Maybe I can go to the park. I tap my good luck song on the wall beside my bed.

I put my feet on the floor and feel the cool wood. Then it is four steps to the table, then around the table, touching the chairs, and then seven steps to the window. I put my cheek against the window, and I can feel the warm sun. Now I am sure I can go to the park, if my sister has time to take me on her way to study.

I take my clothes into the bathroom, and I wash and dress there. Hot water, cold water, soapy water, plain water, loud water, still water. Then I make sure I have turned the faucets tight. I make sure I have buttoned all of my buttons the right way, or my sister will be cross, and maybe not have time to take me to the park.

I tap my good luck song against the door before I open it.

When I open the door, I hear the voices again. My sister's voice is like scissors cutting away at my mother's voice.

I sit at the table, and my mother gives me my breakfast. I breathe on the hot chocolate so I can feel it on my face coming back warm. I drink just a little at a time so I can keep holding the warm cup.

"*Eat while it's hot,*" says my sister to me loudly.

"Does he have to be so slow?" says my sister to my mother in her quiet voice. My sister thinks because I cannot see that maybe I cannot hear very well. She talks loud to me, and soft when she does not want me to hear, but I hear.

"*You spilled,*" says my sister loudly.

"I can't be late," she says in her quiet voice to my mother. "Everybody's always late but me, and I won't be late."

After breakfast I go over to the window again, and when I put my cheek against the glass, it is warmer than before, so today will be a good day. I tap my good luck song against the window.

My sister says she will take me to the park on her way to study. She gives me my jacket and tells me to wait for her outside on the steps.

I go down the outside steps. There are seven steps. Seven is my most magic number. Seven up, seven down, seven up, seven down. I go up and down, waiting for my sister.

My sister comes out. She takes my hand. She walks very fast, but I can still count the steps to the park, and I can still remember the turns. Someday I can go there by myself. I listen to the street noises and try to sort them out.

My sister's hand is not soft. I can feel her nails, little and sharp, like her voice, and I listen to her heels making holes in all the other sounds.

The park seems a long way off.

When we get to the park, we first go to the bench. She waits to make sure I remember my way in the park. Fourteen steps to the bubbler, around the bubbler, twenty steps to the curb.

I go back to the bench. I try to hurry so my sister won't have to wait long and be cross. Now seventeen steps to the telephone booth, four benches on the way, and I touch them all. Then I come back to the bench. My sister puts money in my pocket so I can telephone.

She talks to me and to herself.

"*Filthy park*," she says, and it is as if she were stepping on the words. "No grass. Trees in cages. Since when do benches and old newspapers make a park?" She pulls my jacket to straighten it.

Now she is gone, and I have my morning in the sun.

I try each bench, but mine is still the best one.

I go to the bubbler and press my mouth against the water and feel it on my tongue, soft and warm. I put my finger on the place where the water comes out and walk around and around the bubbler, and then I try to find my bench. It is one of my games. I have many games.

I walk over to the telephone booth, touching the four benches on the way. I stand inside the booth. I feel to see if there is any money in the telephone, but there is none. My sister says I should always check the telephone for money, but I have never found any.

I practice dialing our number so I will be sure I have it right. Then I put my dime in and call. I let it ring two times, and then I hang up and get my dime back. My sister says, that way my mother will know I am all right.

I blow on the glass and it blows back to me. I tap my good luck song on it and go back to my bench.

I play one of my games. I listen to every sound and think if that sound would be able to do something to me, what it would do. Some sounds would scratch me, some would pinch me, some would push me. Some would carry me, some would crush me, and some would rock me.

I am sitting on my bench tapping my good luck song with my shoes when I hear the bells of an ice cream truck. I feel the money in my pocket. I have the dime, and I also have a bigger one. I know I have enough for an ice cream bar.

I walk out to the curb, touching the cages around the trees. I wait until the bells sound near, and I wave.

Part Two

The ice cream man stops. He is near enough for me to touch his cart. I hold out my money.

Now I feel him seeing me, but he does not take my money. "Here," I say, but he still does not take the money from me.

"Guess what?" he says, and his voice is kind and soft as fur. "Every tenth kid wins a free ice cream bar, and you're the lucky one today."

I can feel him getting off his cart and going around to open the place where he keeps his ice cream bars. I can feel him putting one near my hand, and I take it. I start back to my bench.

"You gonna be okay by yourself now?" the ice cream man calls, so I know he is seeing me.

I sit on the bench. I listen for the sound of his cart starting up, and his bells ringing, but I can only hear the other sounds, the regular ones. Then I hear him walking over to my bench.

I am sorry, because I only want to feel the ice cream and see how long I can make it last. I do not want anyone to sit with me, but he is sitting with me now. I am afraid I will spill, and he will see me.

He starts to talk, and his voice is soft as a sweater.

His name is Abram. He tells me about the park.

My sister says the trees are in cages because if they weren't in cages they wouldn't stay in such a terrible park. They'd just get up and go somewhere pretty.

Abram says the trees are in cages to keep them safe so they can grow up to be big and tall. "Like sides on a crib for a baby, keeping him from falling and hurting himself," says Abram.

My sister says the park is ugly and dirty.

Abram says there are a few little bits of paper, and a couple of cans and some bottles, but he says he can squint his eyes and all those things lying around shine like flowers. Abram says you see what you want to see.

My sister says the park is just for poor folks, and that no one would ever come if they had a chance to go anywhere else.

Abram says the park is just for lucky people, like him and me. He says the people who come to this park can see things inside themselves, instead of just what their eyes tell them.

After a while Abram goes away. He says he will come back and look for me tomorrow. I hear his ice cream bells go farther and farther away until I do not hear them anymore.

While I am waiting for my sister to come for me, I fall asleep on the bench.

I have a good dream. I dream that Abram lifts me so I can touch the leaves of a tree. All of the leaves are songs, and they fall around me and cover me. I am warm and soft under the songs.

My sister shakes me awake. "You'll catch cold lying here," she says.

The next day while I am sitting on my bench, I hear the ice cream bells and I walk out to the curb, touching the cages of the trees as I go. Abram gives me an ice cream bar and we walk together back to the bench. I do not have to touch the cages because I am with him.

After I finish my ice cream bar Abram gives me some paper clips so I can feel them in my pocket. He shows me how I can twist them to make little shapes.

After he leaves, I feel them. There are seven paper clips.

That night I dream that someone is gathering in a big net everything in the world that makes

a sound, and I am tumbled in the net with dogs and cars and whistles and buses. I try to get out of the net and my sister shakes me awake.

"Stop thrashing around," she says. "You're all tangled up in the blanket."

The next day Abram brings me a balloon.

I can feel it round and tight. It tugs at the string.

Abram says some balloons are filled with something special that makes them want to fly away, up to the sun, and this balloon is filled with that something special.

He says some people are filled with something special that makes them pull and tug, too, trying to get up and away from where they are.

His voice is like a kitten curled on my shoulder.

He tells me my balloon is red, and he tells me about colors.

He says colors are just like sounds. Some colors are loud, and some colors are soft, and some are big and some are little, and some are sharp and some are tender, just like sounds, just like music.

What is the best color, I wonder?

He says all colors are the same, as far as that goes.

There isn't a best color, says Abram. There isn't a good color or a bad color.

Colors are just on the outside. They aren't important at all. They're just covers for things like a blanket.

Color doesn't mean a thing, says Abram.

When my sister comes, she asks me where I got my balloon.

I tell her about my friend.

I hold on to the string of my balloon while we walk.

When we get home, I tie the string of my balloon to my chair.

I have a bad dream in the night. I dream that my ears are pulling in every sound in the world, so many sounds I cannot breathe. I am choking with the sounds that are pulled into me and I have to keep coughing the sounds away as they come in, or I will smother.

"Here's some stuff for your cold," says my sister.

When I am awake again, I cannot tell if it is morning. I hear noises but they are not the morning noises. My sister has her quiet voice, and I do not hear the little hard sounds of her heels making holes in the morning.

She is wearing slippers. She tells my mother she is not going to go to study today.

There is no hurry about today. I reach for my balloon. The string lies on the chair, and I find the balloon on the floor, small and soft and limp. It does not float. It lies in my hand, tired and sad.

I lie there and listen to the sound of slippers on the kitchen floor.

I tap my good luck song against the wall over and over, but I hear the rain and I know I will not go to the park today.

Tomorrow it will be a nice day. Tomorrow my sister and I will go to the park and find Abram. He will make my balloon as good as new.

Now I walk over to the window and lean my head against it.

The rain taps its song to me against the glass, and I tap back.

Voices

There are songs and sounds in stillness
In the quiet after dark,
Sounds within sounds,
Songs within songs.
There are rhythms in the quiet
And pulses in the night,
Beats within beats,
Drums within drums.

Something calling in the embers,
Something crying in the rocks,
And out beyond the darkness
There are voices in the stars.

—Felice Holman

MR. HARE

Gardell Dano Christensen

The Players

FOX
HARE
TORTOISE
BADGER
SKUNK
BEAVER
SQUIRREL

Act 1

Time: Early one Saturday evening.
Place: Old Log, the animals' meeting place in the woods.

(FOX, HARE, *and* TORTOISE *are talking.*)

Fox. Did you ever hear the story, *The Hare and the Tortoise?*

HARE (*very angry*). Yes, I've heard it. I've heard it so many times I'm sick and tired of it. Everyone knows the story isn't true. Come on, Tortoise. Let's have a race. I'll show you that story isn't true.

FOX. Let's do something different this time. I've got it! Let's have a contest. Do either of you have any friends?

HARE. Of course, lots of them.

TORTOISE. Well, I've only been here two years. So, I guess I can't really say that I have a friend yet. Why?

FOX. Because I would like to have a contest to see which one of you can bring the most friends here to Old Log at this time a week from today.

TORTOISE. Oh, all right. I'll try.

(TORTOISE *crawls slowly away*.)

HARE. That won't be hard for me. I'm sure all my friends will come.

(HARE *hops away quickly*.)

Act 2

Time: The next morning.
Place: The main road in the woods.

(HARE *stops at* BADGER'S *house.*
BADGER *is eating lunch.*)

HARE. Oh, sorry. I didn't know you were eating.

BADGER. Think nothing of it. Pull up a chair and have some lunch with me.

HARE. No, thanks. I'll only be here a minute or two. I'll get right to the point. I'm in a contest in which I have to bring a lot of friends.

BADGER. But, my boy, it takes time to make friends.

HARE. All I have to do is have people come to Old Log next Saturday and say they are my friends.

BADGER. Well, I'm pretty busy, but I'll try to be there.

HARE. Oh, thank you very much. I'll see you next Saturday.

BADGER. Good-by, my friend.

(HARE *stops at* SKUNK'S *house. He rings the bell. There is no answer at first. He rings the bell again.*)

SKUNK. Yes, what is it?

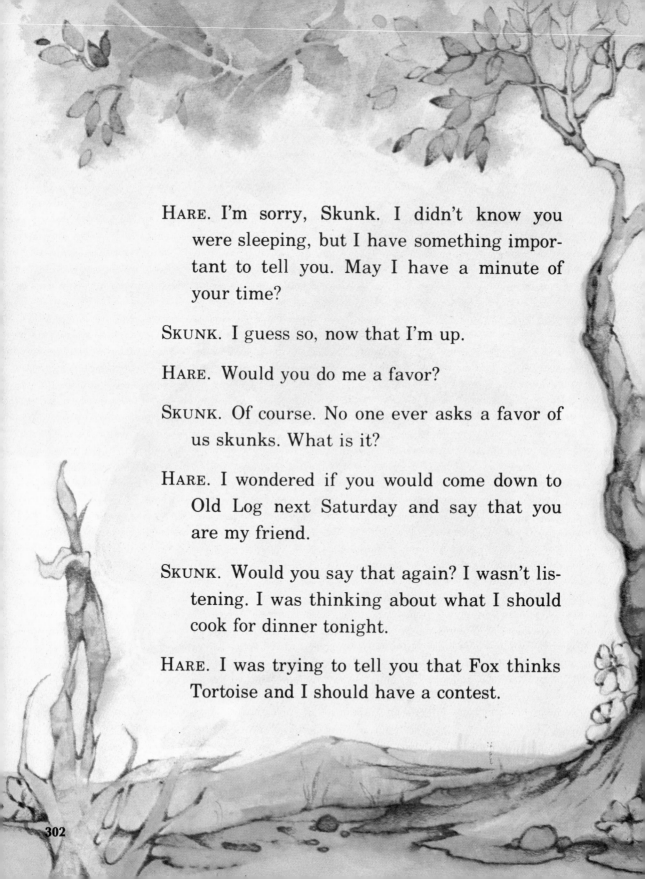

HARE. I'm sorry, Skunk. I didn't know you were sleeping, but I have something important to tell you. May I have a minute of your time?

SKUNK. I guess so, now that I'm up.

HARE. Would you do me a favor?

SKUNK. Of course. No one ever asks a favor of us skunks. What is it?

HARE. I wondered if you would come down to Old Log next Saturday and say that you are my friend.

SKUNK. Would you say that again? I wasn't listening. I was thinking about what I should cook for dinner tonight.

HARE. I was trying to tell you that Fox thinks Tortoise and I should have a contest.

SKUNK. Oh, I love a race! But how can you race
Fox and hope to win?

HARE. No, Skunk. I'm not in a race with Fox.
I'm in a contest with Tortoise.

SKUNK. Oh no, you don't mean it! That isn't fair. Everyone knows Tortoise can't win. Even skunks can run faster than tortoises.

HARE. No! No! No, Skunk. It's not a race. It's a contest! The idea is to see who can get the most friends in a week. I want you to be my friend.

SKUNK. I'll do anything to put that horrible Fox in his place. I don't see how people can stand him. He smells so!

HARE. I have to go now, Skunk, but be sure to be at Old Log next Saturday.

(HARE *goes down the road to the beaver pond.*)

BEAVER *(working on his dam)*. Hello, young fellow, what can I do for you?

HARE. May I talk with you for a minute?

BEAVER. As you know, I'm always busy. I don't have much time to talk.

HARE. I only wanted to tell you that I'm having a contest with Tortoise . . .

BEAVER. A contest! A contest needs a *judge* and everyone knows I am the best judge around here.

HARE. We have a judge. Fox is the judge.

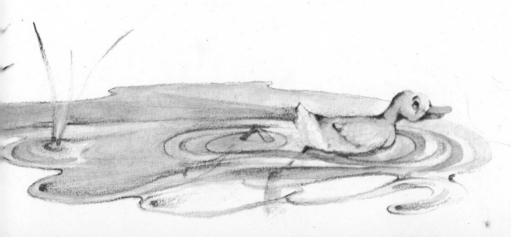

BEAVER. Fox? The judge? Fox is smart, but he's
no judge.

HARE. All I want you to do is come to Old Log
on Saturday and say you are my friend.

BEAVER. It sounds interesting, and I wouldn't
miss something interesting for anything.
But, mind you, I'm a very busy man, and I
don't have time for . . .

HARE. Good-by, Beaver, and thank you.

(HARE *hops down the road.* BEAVER *goes on
working on his dam.*)

Act 3

Time: Saturday afternoon, a week later.
Place: The road to Old Log.

(HARE *hops down the road to* BADGER'S *house.*)

BADGER. What are you doing here, Hare?

HARE. I just wanted to remind you that today is Saturday. You said you would come to Old Log and say you are my friend.

BADGER. But I thought that was all over. You said you wanted to start a friendship, and then you never showed up again. So I made other plans for tonight, and I can't change them now. Come around some other day when you have more time to start a real friendship. I must go in now. It's almost time for lunch.

(BADGER *goes into his house.* HARE *hops down the road to* SKUNK'S *house.* SQUIRREL *opens the door.*)

SQUIRREL. You won't find anyone home today. The Skunks went to visit some friends. Is there anything I can do?

HARE. Yes, you can come to Old Log tonight and say you are my friend.

SQUIRREL. Oh, I can't come tonight. All the squirrels are meeting to find places for our winter supplies.

(SQUIRREL *closes the door.* HARE *hops down to the beaver pond where* BEAVER *is working.*)

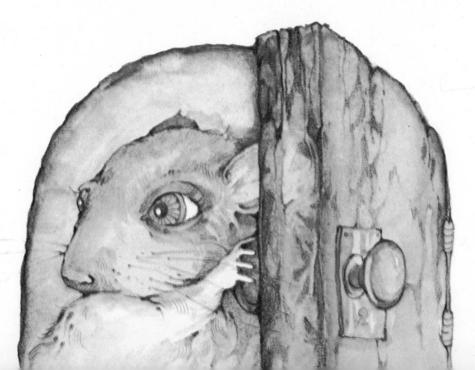

HARE. Are you coming to Old Log?

BEAVER. What is this all about?

HARE. You promised to come to Old Log to-night and say you are my friend.

BEAVER. You said you didn't need a judge. I don't have the time to hang around Old Log like the other animals. I'm sure you will have many friends who will be there. You won't miss me at all. Now, if I were the judge . . .

(HARE *hops down the road*).

Act 4

Time: Saturday evening.
Place: Old Log.

(HARE *comes to Old Log and finds* Fox *waiting for him.*)

Fox. No friends, I see. But you notice there is no Tortoise either. So maybe you haven't lost.

(TORTOISE *crawls slowly down the road toward Old Log. Another tortoise is with him.*)

TORTOISE. I want you to meet my friend. He is the only one I had time to see. We found there were so many interesting things to talk about, the week was gone before we knew it. I don't know if I have made a good showing for the contest, but at least I have a good friend now.

(HARE *and* FOX *sit down on the log. Neither one says a word.*)

The Wisest Man in the World

Benjamin Elkin

Part One

In days of old, so it is said, a little bee flew into the castle of the great King Solomon. The angry guards ran to trap it. But the bee got away from them and flew to the King for safety.

Now this King was the wisest man in the world. So wise that he could speak the language of every living thing.

"O King," said the bee. *"Spare me today that I may live to serve you tomorrow."*

King Solomon smiled to think that this tiny bee could ever hope to serve a mighty king. But he drew the curtains and gently let the bee go with his own hand.

"Go in peace," he said. "I want nothing in return."

Through the open curtains the King saw a great caravan. There were many animals wearing jewels and gold. And at the head of the caravan rode the proud and beautiful Queen of Sheba.

The Queen and her caravan had come far across the wide desert to visit the King.

The King, dressed in his royal robes, was seated on his throne. It was a magnificent throne. On each side of the six steps leading to the throne stood two golden lions and two golden eagles. These golden lions and eagles allowed no one to lie to the King. If anyone dared to tell a lie, the lions roared and the eagles screeched.

When the Queen of Sheba entered, she could not hide her surprise at King Solomon's magnificent throne.

"May the King live forever," she said. *"I come as a true friend."*

At once, the golden lions roared and the eagles screeched. For the Queen had told a lie. She did not come as a true friend. But she knew nothing of the lions and eagles. So she bowed politely, thinking this was a royal greeting.

The Queen of Sheba had been jealous of King Solomon for a long time. During her visit she was hoping to shame him before his own people and even before the whole world.

During the next few days the Queen of Sheba did her best to show that King Solomon was not really wise.

She asked him riddles, but he answered all of them.

She brought him a large jewel with a winding hole through it. Then she asked him to draw a thread through it.

King Solomon only smiled and sent for a silkworm. The worm crawled through the hole, drawing a silk thread through it.

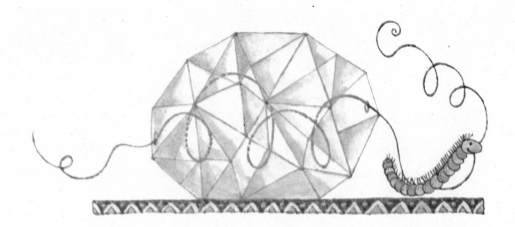

Another time, the Queen sent in sixty little boys and girls, all dressed alike. "If you please," she said, "tell me from your throne which are boys and which are girls."

The King sent for bowls of water to put before each child. Then he bid them wash their faces.

The boys splashed water on their faces while the girls dabbed the water with their fingertips. And so the King could easily tell them apart.

Once the King and Queen saw that a little
dog had fallen into a deep pool. The water was
so low that the dog could not be reached. King
Solomon threw a log into the water for the dog
to climb on.

"I would not have done so," said the Queen.
"It is better to drown quickly than to die slowly
of hunger." And she was happy, thinking that
at last the King had done something that was
not wise.

But King Solomon did not stop to answer.
He showed his men how to block the nearby
stream with rocks. As the stream spilled over
into the pool, the water rose higher and higher.
Soon the log floated up within reach, and the
dog was safely lifted out.

Part Two

That night the Queen of Sheba met with her councilors. "So far we have had no success," she said, "and tomorrow will be our last chance. The King has invited people from many lands to a banquet in my honor. For this banquet we *must* find a trick that will show them that King Solomon is not wise, but a fool."

"Such a trick we have found," said the Queen's councilors.

From King Solomon's garden the councilors plucked a flower. Then they ordered their craftsmen to make ninety-nine false flowers exactly like it. And then they placed just one fresh flower among the ninety-nine false ones. The Queen of Sheba herself could not point out the real one.

"Well done," said the Queen. "King Solomon will surely mistake a false flower for a fresh one from his own garden. By tonight he will be a joke among all his people."

One of the King's servants heard this and told the King. But King Solomon had become so proud and so sure of himself that he did not worry about it.

319

"It matters not," he said. "It suits me well that they should show how wise I am before all my people. I fear not what they may do."

That night the castle shined with lights as hundreds of people came to honor King Solomon and the Queen of Sheba.

At just the right time, the Queen said, "O King, my craftsmen wish that you judge their work. Among these flowers only one comes from your garden. The others were made by my craftsmen in your honor. Won't you pick out your own flower and let my craftsmen know how real theirs look? Smell them. Touch them," she told the King.

At first the King was sure that he could find the real one. But they all smelled the same. He felt them, but they all felt the same. Maybe this was a trick, and *all* the flowers were false. Then he would be wrong no matter which one he picked.

Never had King Solomon believed he could be tricked. As he stood there, the people began to whisper. "What is wrong? Can't the King pick out a flower from his own garden? Maybe he is not so wise after all!"

Then King Solomon felt something tickling his hand. A little bee had landed there. "I am here to help you," whispered the bee.

It flew low over the flowers. Then it crawled into the one flower that had honey inside.

No one else had seen the little bee. King Solomon leaned over and plucked the one flower with the bee in it, the one flower that had grown in his garden.

"Yes," said the King, "your craftsmen do very fine work. But the false cannot be true. The others are false, and this one is true."

The Queen looked at the flower and saw that it was the single real flower.

Later in the quiet of his rooms, King Solomon thought of the little bee that had served him so well. He bowed his head. "I have been too proud," he said. "No one is so great that he needs no help. And no one is so small that he cannot give it."

Surely, wisdom is given
  to all living things,
And the tiniest creatures
  are teachers of kings.

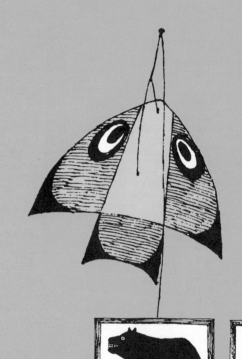

Florence Parry Heide

The Shrinking of Treehorn

Something very strange was happening to Tree-horn.

The first thing he noticed was that he couldn't reach the shelf in his closet that he had always been able to reach before, the one where he hid his candy bars and bubble gum.

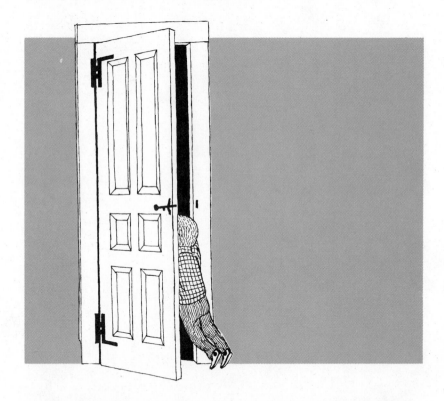

Then he noticed that his clothes were getting too big.

"My trousers are all stretching or something," said Treehorn to his mother. "I'm tripping on them all the time."

"That's too bad, dear," said his mother, looking into the oven. "I do hope this cake isn't going to fall," she said.

"And my sleeves come down way below my hands," said Treehorn. "So my shirts must be stretching, too."

"Think of that," said Treehorn's mother. "I just don't know why this cake isn't rising the way it should. Mrs. Abernale's cakes are *always* nice. They *always* rise."

Treehorn started out of the kitchen. He tripped on his trousers, which indeed did seem to be getting longer and longer.

At dinner that night Treehorn's father said, "Do sit up, Treehorn. I can hardly see your head."

"I *am* sitting up," said Treehorn. "This is as far up as I come. I think I must be shrinking or something."

"I'm sorry my cake didn't turn out very well," said Treehorn's mother.

"It's very nice, dear," said Treehorn's father politely.

By this time Treehorn could hardly see over the top of the table.

"Sit up, dear," said Treehorn's mother.

"I *am* sitting up," said Treehorn. "It's just that I'm shrinking."

"What, dear?" asked his mother.

"I'm shrinking. Getting smaller," said Treehorn.

"If you want to pretend you're shrinking, that's all right," said Treehorn's mother, "as long as you don't do it at the table."

"But I *am* shrinking," said Treehorn.

"Don't argue with your mother, Treehorn," said Treehorn's father.

"He does look a little smaller," said Treehorn's mother, looking at Treehorn. "Maybe he *is* shrinking."

"Nobody shrinks," said Treehorn's father.

"Well, I'm shrinking," said Treehorn. "Look at me."

Treehorn's father looked at Treehorn.

"Why, you're shrinking," said Treehorn's father. "Look, Emily, Treehorn is shrinking. He's much smaller than he used to be."

"Oh, dear," said Treehorn's mother. "First it was the cake, and now it's this. Everything happens at once."

"I *thought* I was shrinking," said Treehorn, and he went into the den to turn on the television set.

Treehorn liked to watch television. Now he lay on his stomach in front of the television set and watched one of his favorite programs. He had fifty-six favorite programs.

During the commercials, Treehorn always listened to his mother and father talking together, unless they were having a boring conversation. If they were having a boring conversation, he listened to the commercials.

Now he listened to his mother and father.

"He really is getting smaller," said Treehorn's mother. "What will we do? What will people say?"

"Why, they'll say he's getting smaller," said Treehorn's father. He thought for a moment. "I wonder if he's doing it on purpose. Just to be different."

"Why would he want to be different?" asked Treehorn's mother.

Treehorn started listening to the commercial.

The next morning Treehorn was still smaller. His regular clothes were much too big to wear. He rummaged around in his closet until he found some of his last year's clothes. They were much too big, too, but he put them on and rolled up the pants and rolled up the sleeves and went down to breakfast.

Treehorn liked cereal for breakfast. But mostly he liked cereal boxes. He always read every single thing on the cereal box while he was eating breakfast. And he always sent in for the things the cereal box said he could send for.

In a box in his closet Treehorn saved all of the things he had sent in for from cereal box tops. He had puzzles and special rings and flashlights and pictures of all of the presidents and pictures of all of the baseball players. And he had pictures of scenes suitable for framing, which he had never framed because he didn't like them very much. And he had all kinds of games and pens and models.

Today on the cereal box was a very special offer of a very special whistle that only dogs could hear. Treehorn did not have a dog, but he thought it would be nice to have a whistle that dogs could hear, even if *he* couldn't hear it. Even if *dogs* couldn't hear it, it would be nice to have a whistle, just to have it.

He decided to eat all of the cereal in the box so he could send in this morning for the whistle. His mother never let him send in for anything until he had eaten all of the cereal in the box.

Treehorn filled in all of the blank spaces for his name and address and then he went to get his money out of the piggy bank on the kitchen counter, but he couldn't reach it. .

"I certainly *am* getting smaller," thought Treehorn. He climbed up on a chair and got the piggy bank and shook out a dime.

His mother was cleaning the refrigerator. "You know how I hate to have you climb up on the chairs, dear," she said. She went into the living room to dust.

Treehorn put the piggy bank in the bottom kitchen drawer.

"That way I can get it no matter *how* little I get," he thought.

He found an envelope and put a stamp on it and put the dime and the box top in so he could mail the letter on the way to school. The mailbox was right next to the bus stop.

It was hard to walk to the bus stop because his shoes kept slipping off, but he got there in plenty of time, shuffling. He couldn't reach the mailbox slot to put the letter in, so he handed the letter to one of his friends, Moshie, and asked him to put it in. Moshie put it in. "How come you can't mail it yourself, stupid?" asked Moshie.

"Because I'm shrinking," explained Treehorn. "I'm shrinking and I'm too little to reach the mail-box."

"That's a stupid thing to do," said Moshie. "You're *always* doing stupid things, but that's the *stupidest*."

When Treehorn tried to get on the school bus, everyone was pushing and shoving. The bus driver said, "All the way back in the bus, step all the way back." Then he saw Treehorn trying to climb onto the bus.

"Let that little kid on," said the bus driver.

Treehorn was helped onto the bus. The bus driver said, "You can stay right up here next to me if you want to, because you're so little."

"It's me, Treehorn," said Treehorn to his friend the bus driver.

The bus driver looked down at Treehorn. "You do look like Treehorn, at that," he said. "Only smaller. Treehorn isn't that little."

"I am Treehorn. I'm just getting smaller," said Treehorn.

"Nobody gets smaller," said the bus driver. "You must be Treehorn's kid brother. What's your name?"

"Treehorn," said Treehorn.

"First time I ever heard of a family naming two boys the same name," said the bus driver. "Guess they couldn't think of any other name, once they thought of Treehorn."

Treehorn said nothing.

When he went into class, his teacher said, "Nursery school is down at the end of the hall, honey."

"I'm Treehorn," said Treehorn.

"If you're Treehorn, why are you so small?" asked the teacher.

"Because I'm shrinking," said Treehorn. "I'm getting smaller."

"Well, I'll let it go for today," said his teacher. "But see that it's taken care of before tomorrow. We don't shrink in this class."

After recess, Treehorn was thirsty, so he went down the hall to the water bubbler. He couldn't reach it, and he tried to jump up high enough. He still couldn't get a drink, but he kept jumping up and down, trying.

His teacher walked by. "Why, Treehorn," she said. "That isn't like you, jumping up and down in the hall. Just because you're shrinking, it does not mean you have special privileges. What if all the children in the *school* started jumping up and down in the halls? I'm afraid you'll have to go to the Principal's office, Treehorn."

So Treehorn went to the Principal's office.

"I'm supposed to see the Principal," said Tree-horn to the lady in the Principal's outer office.

"It's a very busy day," said the lady. "Please check here on this form the reason you have to see him. That will save time. Be sure to put your name down, too. That will save time. And write clearly. That will save time."

Treehorn looked at the form:

CHECK REASON YOU HAVE TO SEE PRINCIPAL (that will save time)
- [ ] *1. Talking in class*
- [ ] *2. Chewing gum in class*
- [ ] *3. Talking back to teacher*
- [ ] *4. Unexcused absence*
- [ ] *5. Unexcused illness*
- [ ] *6. Unexcused behavior*

There were many things to check, but Treehorn couldn't find one that said "Being Too Small to Reach the Water Bubbler." He finally wrote in "SHRINKING."

When the lady said he could see the Principal, Treehorn went into the Principal's office with his form.

The Principal looked at the form, and then he looked at Treehorn. Then he looked at the form again.

"I can't read this," said the Principal. "It looks like SHIRKING. You're not SHIRKING, are you, Treehorn? We can't have any shirkers here, you know. We're a team, and we all have to do our very best."

"It says SHRINKING," said Treehorn. "I'm shrinking."

"Shrinking, eh?" said the Principal. "Well, now, I'm very sorry to hear that, Treehorn. You were right to come to me. That's what I'm here for. To guide. Not to punish, but to guide. To guide all the members of my team. To solve all their problems."

"But I don't have any problems," said Treehorn. "I'm just shrinking."

"Well, I want you to know I'm right here when you need me, Treehorn," said the Principal, "and I'm glad I was here to help you. A team is only as good as its coach, eh?"

The Principal stood up. "Goodbye, Treehorn. If you have any more problems, come straight to me, and I'll help you again. A problem isn't a problem once it's solved, right?"

By the end of the day Treehorn was still smaller.

At the dinner table that night he sat on several cushions so he could be high enough to see over the top of the table.

"He's still shrinking," sniffed Treehorn's mother. "Heaven knows I've *tried* to be a good mother."

"Maybe we should call a doctor," said Treehorn's father.

"I did," said Treehorn's mother. "I called every doctor in the Yellow Pages. But no one knew anything about shrinking problems."

She sniffed again. "Maybe he'll just keep getting smaller and smaller until he disappears."

"No one disappears," said Treehorn's father positively.

"That's right, they don't," said Treehorn's mother more cheerfully. "But no one shrinks, either," she said after a moment. "Finish your carrots, Treehorn."

The next morning Treehorn was so small he had to jump out of bed. On the floor under the bed was a game he'd pushed under there and forgotten about. He walked under the bed to look at it.

It was one of the games he'd sent in for from a cereal box. He had started playing it a couple of days ago, but he hadn't had a chance to finish it because his mother had called him to come right downstairs that minute and have his breakfast or he'd be late for school.

Treehorn looked at the cover of the box:

THE *BIG* GAME
FOR KIDS TO GROW ON
IT'S TREMENDOUS! IT'S DIFFERENT!
IT'S FUN! IT'S EASY! IT'S COLOSSAL!
PLAY IT WITH FRIENDS!
PLAY IT ALONE!
Complete with Spinner, Board, Pieces,
and—!
COMPLETE INSTRUCTIONS!

The game was called THE *BIG* GAME FOR KIDS TO GROW ON.

Treehorn sat under the bed to finish playing the game.

He always liked to finish things, even if they were boring. Even if he was watching a boring program on TV, he always watched it right to the end. Games were the same way. He'd finish this one now. Where had he left off? He remembered he'd just had to move his piece back seven spaces on the board when his mother had called him.

He was so small now that the only way he could move the spinner was by kicking it, so he kicked it. It stopped at number 4. That meant he could move his piece ahead four spaces on the board.

The only way he could move the piece forward now was by carrying it, so he carried it. It was pretty heavy. He walked along the board to the fourth space. It said CONGRATULATIONS, AND UP YOU GO: ADVANCE THIRTEEN SPACES.

Treehorn started to carry his piece forward the thirteen spaces, but the piece seemed to be getting smaller. Or else *he* was getting *bigger*. That was it, he *was* getting bigger, because the bottom of the bed was getting close to his head. He pulled the game out from under the bed to finish playing it.

He kept moving the piece forward, but he didn't have to carry it any longer. In fact, he seemed to be getting bigger and bigger with each space he landed in.

"Well, I don't want to get *too* big," thought Treehorn. So he moved the piece ahead slowly from one space to the next, getting bigger with each space, until he was his own regular size again. Then he put the spinner and the pieces and the instructions and the board back in the box for THE *BIG* GAME FOR KIDS TO GROW ON and put it in his closet. If he ever wanted to get bigger or smaller he could play it again, even if it *was* a pretty boring game.

Treehorn went down for breakfast and started to read the new cereal box. It said you could send for a hundred balloons. His mother was cleaning the living room. She came into the kitchen to get a dust rag.

"Don't put your elbows on the table while you're eating, dear," she said.

"Look," said Treehorn. "I'm my own size now. My own regular size."

"That's nice, dear," said Treehorn's mother. "It's a very nice size, I'm sure, and if I were you I wouldn't shrink anymore. Be sure to tell your father when he comes home tonight. He'll be so pleased." She went back to the living room and started to dust and vacuum.

That night Treehorn was watching TV. As he reached over to change channels, he noticed that his hand was bright green. He looked in the mirror that was hanging over the television set. His face was green. His ears were green. His hair was green. He was green all over.

Treehorn sighed. "I don't think I'll tell anyone," he thought to himself. "If I don't say anything, they won't notice."

Treehorn's mother came in. "Do turn the volume down a little, dear," she said. "Your father and I are having the Smedleys over to play bridge. Do comb your hair before they come, won't you, dear," said his mother as she walked back to the kitchen.

Glossary

This glossary gives the pronunciations and meanings of some of the words used in this book.

The pronunciation is shown just after the word in this way: able (ā′ bl). The letters and signs are pronounced as shown in the words listed below.

If the word has more than one syllable, as in the example, a heavy accent mark ′ is placed after the syllable that receives the heaviest stress.

PRONUNCIATION KEY

a	hat	i	it	p	paper	v	very
ā	face	ī	ice	r	run	w	will
ã	care	j	jam	s	say	y	yes
ä	father	k	kind	sh	she	z	zoo
b	bad	l	land	t	tell	zh	treasure
ch	child	m	me	th	thin		
d	did	n	no	ŦH	then		
e	let	ng	long	u	cut	ə stands for	
ē	be	o	hot	u̇	pull		a in about
ėr	her	ō	open	ü	June		e in given
f	fat	ô	or	ū	use		i in family
g	go	oi	oil				o in button
h	he	ou	out				u in walrus

A

acrobat (ak′ rə bat) someone who can walk on tightropes, swing on trapezes, and do other such acts

address (ə dres′) the place where someone's mail is to be sent or where he lives: *Write your address on the envelope.*

African (af′ rə kən) coming from or having to do with Africa, one of the seven continents of the world

Alaska (ə las′ kə) the largest state of the United States

Andersen (an′ dər sən), Hans Christian (hanz kris′ chən) writer of fairy tales, born in the country of Denmark

armor (är′ mər) a suit of metal worn to prevent injury in fighting, especially by knights of old

arrow (ar′ ō) a slender stick with a pointed head, which is shot from a bow

ashore (ə shôr′) on the shore; on land

audience (ôd′ ē əns) listeners; people who have gathered to watch and hear a show or concert

August (ô′ gəst) eighth month of the year; one of the summer months

B

backstage (bak′ stāj′) behind the stage

badger (baj′ r) a gray-furred animal that lives underground

banquet (bang′ kwit) a big feast

bar (bär) ice cream or candy shaped like a bar (longer than wide)

bay (bā) a body of water protected on all sides but one by land and joined to the sea or ocean: *The ship found a safe place in the bay.*

beam (bēm) a ray of light

blanket (blang′ kit) a covering, usually woven from woolen thread

blindfold (blīnd′ fōld′) **1.** to cover the eyes with a piece of cloth. **2.** a covering for the eyes

booth (büth) **1.** at a fair, a small room in which goods are shown or sold. **2.** a small closed room for a telephone or some other device

boring (bôr′ ing) dull; not interesting; tiresome

bravo (brä′ vō) wonderful; well done

bubbler (bub′ lər) a drinking-water fountain

bulldozer (bul′ doz′ r) a powerful tractor used to clear land and move earth for buildings and roads

---

hat, fāce, cãre, fäther, let, bē, hėr, it, īce, hot, ōpen, ôr, oil, out, cut, pull, Jüne, ūse, thin, ŦHen; ə stands for a in about, e in given, i in family, o in button, u in walrus.

bushland (bùsh' land) the wilds; a forest

Bushmen (bùsh' mən) hunters that once lived in the bushland of South Africa

business (biz' nəs) **1.** work; a way of making a living. **2.** money made from selling goods or services: *In the summer Ben's hot dog stand does a good business.* **3.** a matter of interest: *We talked about class business.*

C

Canada (kan' ə də) the country lying on the northern border of the United States

canyon (kan' yən) a deep valley between steep mountainsides

cape (kāp) a coat without sleeves or armholes, worn around the shoulders

caravan (kar' ə van) a long line of people, animals, and wagons traveling together for safety across desert or wild country and often carrying goods to sell

cart (kärt) a wagon with two wheels

cereal (sir' ē l) a breakfast food made from some kind of grain

chains (chānz) a kind of rope made of metal loops linked together

channels (chan' əlz) in TV, the stations carrying the programs

Christmas (kris' məs) December 25, the holy day celebrating the birth of Jesus Christ

claim (klām) **1.** the right to own or demand something. **2.** to demand something as one's right

clues (klüz) hints; keys to solving a mystery; tracks

coach (kōch) a teacher or trainer

colonel (kėr' nəl) an army officer

conversation (kon' vər sā' shən) talk

Copenhagen (kō' pən hā' gən) the capital city of the country of Denmark

councilors (koun' səl ərz) people who are asked for advice

counter (koun' tər) a shelf or table

court (kôrt) the place where a ruler and his followers live

craftsmen (krafts' mən) men skilled in a line of work or art

crayfish (krā' fish') a shellfish that looks like a small lobster

crocodile (krok' ə dīl) a large lizard that lives in warm waters and has a thick skin, powerful jaws, and a long body and tail

cropped (kropt) cut short

curb (kėrb) the edge of the pavement; the raised edge along a street

D

dabbed (dabd) patted with something

dawn (dôn) daybreak; the first light of day; the beginning of day

design (di zīn′) a pattern; a plan

dialing (dī′ l ing) turning the part of a telephone used in making calls

dock (dok) a large float or pier to which boats or seaplanes may be tied

drag (drag) to pull along the ground

drawbridge (drô′ brij′) a bridge that may be raised and lowered to let boats pass

dune (dün) a hill or mound of sand

E

eagles (ēg′ əlz) large, powerful birds

east (ēst) **1.** the direction in which the sun rises. **2.** when written with capital *E*, the part of a country that lies to the east

emperor (em′ pər ər) in some countries, the name of the ruler

evergreens (ev′ər grēnz) trees or bushes that stay green all year

F

Fairbanks (fãr′ bangks) a city in the state of Alaska

false (fôls) not true

faucets (fô′ sits) water taps

favor (fā′ vər) an act of kindness; a good turn: *Do me a favor.*

fellow (fel′ ō) a friend; a companion

filthy (fil′ thē) very dirty

fingerprints (fing′ gər prints′) the markings of the fingertips on something: *The thief left his fingerprints all over the desk.*

flashlight (flash′ līt′) a small light powered by batteries and able to be carried around

flock (flok) a gathering of animals

form (fôrm) **1.** a model. **2.** a printed sheet with blank spaces for writing certain information

foundation (foun dā′ shən) the part on which everything else rests

frail (frāl) weak; not strong

G

glided (glīd′ id) moved smoothly, with grace and ease

government (guv′ ərn ment) people and groups that make the laws of a country and carry them out

gym (jim) a large hall or room for indoor games and exercises

---

hat, fāce, cãre, fäther, let, bē, hėr, it, īce, hot, ōpen, ôr, oil, out, cut, pull, Jūne, ūse, thin, ŦHen; ə stands for a in about, e in given, i in family, o in button, u in walrus.

H

handcuffs (hand′ kufs′) iron bracelets or rings that may be locked around the wrists to keep someone from using his hands

harbor (här′ bər) a place where boats may dock

hare (hãr) an animal that looks like a rabbit but is much larger

haunted (hôn′ tid) visited often by ghosts

heap (hēp) a hill; a pile

herd (hėrd) a large band or group of some animals

hermit (hėr′ mit) someone who lives by himself, away from others

Houdini (hü dē′ nē) Harry (har′ ē) a famous American stage magician

I

India (in′ dē ə) a country in southern Asia

Italy (it′ l ē) one of the countries in the southern part of Europe

J

judge (juj) **1.** someone who hears and settles cases of law. **2.** someone who decides on the winner of a contest. **3.** someone who decides on the worth or value of something. **4.** to decide or settle a contest

K

knight (nīt) in early times, a title given by a king or queen to someone who had passed several tests of bravery and who promised to spend his life defending the weak and serving the king

L

lance (lans) a long spear carried by knights

lawn (lôn) land covered with grass

lawn mower (lôn mō′ r) a machine for cutting grass

lions (lī′ ənz) large, strong wild animals of the cat family, found in Africa and Asia

lobby (lob′ ē) a hall leading to the main room or rooms of a building, especially of a theater, museum, or hotel: *We met in the museum lobby.*

looms (lümz) machines for weaving threads into cloth

M

magician (mə ji′ shən) one who does magic; a skilled performer of tricks

mainland (mān′ land) a large body of land that is not an island but lies off an island or islands

makeup (māk′ up′) paints, powder, and dress used by actors to play their parts

man-sized (man' sīzd) large enough for a man

marble (mär' bl) a small hard ball used in the game of marbles

mat (mat) a small rug woven from straw, rope, vines, or pieces of cloth

midget (mij' it) **1.** very small. **2.** one who is very small

miner (mīn' ər) someone who works in a mine or who digs for rocks that contain such metals as gold or silver

minister (min' is tər) in some countries, the director of a branch of government

model (mod' l) a small copy of an object

mow (mō) to cut

mule (mūl) an animal half burro, half horse

mysteriously (mis tēr' ē əs lē) without being seen or understood: *The eagle had returned just as mysteriously as it had disappeared.*

N

national (nash' ən l) belonging to a nation: *Thanksgiving is a national holiday in the United States.*

nature (nā' chər) all things in our surroundings except those made by man

nursery (nėr' sər ē) a school or place for small children

O

Odense (ō' den sə) a city in Denmark

office (ôf' is) a job or position, especially in government

officer (ôf' ə sər) **1.** in the army, someone who commands others. **2.** someone who holds an office. **3.** a policeman; someone who keeps the peace in a town

ordinary (ôrd' n er' ē) not special

oxygen (ok' sə jən) one of the gasses that make up the air and without which plants and animals cannot live

P

palm (päm) **1.** the inside of the hand between the fingers and the wrist. **2.** a palm tree and/or leaf tree that grows in warm parts

parkmaster (pärk' mas' tər) a director of a park

patterns (pat' ərnz) designs

peace (pēs) **1.** having to do with keeping order: *A policeman is a peace officer.* **2.** without danger of war. **3.** order; quiet

peppermint (pep' ər mint) **1.** an oil that is added to candy to give it a sharp flavor. **2.** flavored by peppermint oil

hat, fāce, cãre, fäther, let, bē, hėr, it, īce, hot, ōpen, ôr, oil, out, cut, pùll, Jūne, ūse, thin, ŦHen; ə stands for a in about, e in given, i in family, o in button, u in walrus.

perch (pėrch) **1.** anything on which a bird can rest. **2.** to rest as birds do

performer (pər fôrm' ər) an actor; a player

plain (plān) clear; easy to see or understand

plastic (plas' tik) made of a man-made material that can be molded

poison (poi' zən) **1.** something that may harm or even kill. **2.** carrying poison

positively (poz' ə tiv lē) for sure; without doubt

post (pōst) in the wilderness, a trading station or store where settlers or trappers may get supplies in return for furs or other goods

powwow (pou' wou') North American Indian word for meeting

prairie (prãr' ē) a large area of flat or rolling grassland

pretend (pri tend') to make believe

prints (prints) marks made by stamping or pressing on something with the feet or fingertips; tracks left by animals

privileges (priv' ə lə jez) special favors or rights

procession (prə sesh' n) a parade

puppets (pup' its) dolls moved by wires or strings from behind or above a stage

purpose (pėr' pəs) **1.** a plan or an aim. **2.** with *on*, not by accident or chance

rafters (raf' tərz) beams that hold up a roof

rail (rāl) a bar of a fence or a bar that forms a fence, as on a stairway

recess (ri' ses) time out from work

refreshments (ri fresh' mənts) food or drink served at a meeting or party

rehearse (ri hėrs') to practice

riddles (rid' əlz) puzzling questions

ruin (rü' n) that which is left of an old building or buildings

rummaged (rum' ijd) looked around by moving things about

sash (sash) a long strip of cloth worn around the waist

seaweed (sē' wēd) plants that grow in the sea

shack (shak) a rundown house; a hut

Sheba (shē' bə) in olden times, a kingdom in Arabia

shingle (shing' gəl) **1.** a small piece of wood used as a covering for roofs. **2.** to put shingles on the roof

shirking (shėrk' ing) avoiding or getting out of doing work

shrinking (shringk' ing) growing smaller

shuffling (shuf' ling) dragging one's feet

silkworm (silk′ wėrm′) a caterpillar that spins a silk cocoon, or case, to lie in while it turns into a moth

single (sing′ gəl) one

sink (singk) **1.** a basin or tub joined to a pipe and used for washing dishes. **2.** to go down

skunk (skungk) a black and white striped animal that gives off a strong smell when afraid or in danger

smother (smuth′ ər) **1.** not able to breathe. **2.** to make unable to breathe

snails (snālz) small, slow-moving animals with soft bodies protected by shells

sniffed (snift) **1.** breathed through the nose, trying not to cry. **2.** smelled

snug (snug) warm; comfortable

Solomon (sol′ ə mən) king of ancient Israel, famous for his wise acts

spaceship (spās′ ship′) an aircraft powered by rockets that can send it into outer space

spider web (spī′dər web) a net spun by a spider in order to trap insects

splint (splint) a piece of wood used to hold a broken bone in place

spotlight (spot′ līt′) a lamp used to throw a bright light on a stage

squaw (skwô) an Indian word for woman; wife

squint (skwint) to partly close the eyes

stake (stāk) to mark with small stakes; to mark the boundaries of a claim on land

stilts (stilts) two poles with steps for the feet

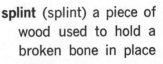

stretching (strech′ ing) growing larger

stupid (stü′ pid) dull; dumb

supplies (sə plīz′) things needed

T

tape recorder (tāp ri kôrd′ ər) a machine that makes a copy of sounds on plastic ribbon or tape

theater (thē′ ə tər) place where plays are put on or where movies are shown

thirst (thėrst) a strong desire for something to drink

thrashing (thrash′ ing) moving about; tossing and turning

tightropes (tīt′ rōps′) ropes or wires pulled tightly above the ground on which acrobats perform

hat, fāce, cãre, fäther, let, bē, hėr, it, īce, hot, ōpen, ôr, oil, out, cut, pùll, Jüne, ūse, thin, ŦHen; ə stands for a in about, e in given, i in family, o in button, u in walrus.

topsoil (top′ soil) rich soil; the top part of the earth where crops are planted

tortoise (tôr′ təs) a land turtle

tower (tou′ ər) a high building, often part of a castle

trapeze (tra pēz′) a high swing on which acrobats perform

tripping (trip′ ing) stumbling; falling over

tugs (tugz) pulls

tunnel (tun′ l) an underground passage or walkway

tusks (tusks) on some animals, long pointed teeth: *Elephants and walruses have tusks.*

U

uproar (up′ rôr′) a loud noise; excitement; a noisy disturbance

V

vacation (vā kā′ shən) a holiday; time off from work or school

vine (vīn) a plant whose stem grows along the ground or up a wall or fence

volleyball (vol′ ē bôl′) a game in which a ball is hit by hand back and forth across a net without letting it touch the ground

volume (vol′ yùm) loudness of sound

W

walkie-talkie (wôk′ ē tôk′ ē) a small radio that may be carried about to send or receive messages

wampum (wom′ pəm) beads or shells which North American Indians used for money

water hole (wô′tər hōl) a natural hollow in the earth in which there is water

weathered (weth′ ərd) worn by the sun, wind, and rain

weave (wēv) to make cloth out of thread

web (web) something woven to trap, such as a spider web

webbed (webd) **1.** like a spider web. **2.** having toes joined by a skin: *Ducks have webbed feet.*

wigwam (wig′ wom) an Indian hut used by many North American Indians in the East and made of poles covered with skins

wires (wīrz) in a circus, the high tight-ropes upon which acrobats perform

Y

yellow pages (yel′ō pāj′ iz) the part of the telephone book in which addresses and phone numbers of services and businesses are listed